Run!

Las Vegas

CLARK KENT

This book is dedicated to the memory of Lonnie D. Wells the Smoothest brother I ever knew. May your soul rest in peace until the Day of Judgment.

Page left intentionally blank

Table of Contents   Page

Chapter 1

What Happens in Vegas

I got off of the plane and walked through the terminal to collect my bags then headed to the rental car pick up area. The airport was crowded for a Wednesday afternoon. Crowds of people getting off of planes and lines of people getting on planes to leave Vegas were everywhere. I decided to stop at Sammy's Beach Bar and Grill in terminal one. It was definitely a colorful bar if I had ever seen one. Bright red and neon green bar chairs sat around a blue bar. Surfboards in every color hung above the bar. I felt like I was in a gay version of Chucky Cheese. It was definitely not what I was looking for.

I walked back out into the airport in search of something with more of a relaxed atmosphere. I found another place called Villa Fresh Italian Kitchen but it looked a little too relaxed. I decided to just go to the rental car area to get my car.

They pulled my rental car to the curb and popped the trunk for me to put my bags in. It was an all white Chrysler 300. It was nice. I signed off for the rental and pulled of onto Wayne Newton Boulevard looking for Sunset. I really didn't have much of a destination other than finding my hotel. I laughed to myself thinking about how much Jersey would have loved being here. It looked like a combination of Hollywood and New York in the middle of the desert. It even had the Statue of Liberty.

On Sunset I turned and drove some more until I ended up turning onto Las Vegas Boulevard. I drove past the big Welcome to Las Vegas sign. I saw the big cowboy sign waving at me in front of an old casino. While I was stopped at a red light I watched as tourists walked up and down the street on both sides. I remembered how I felt the first time I saw Hollywood Boulevard.

The casinos and hotels were all big tall buildings that had big signs and bright lights. I saw the Four Seasons and Mandalay Bay as I drove on then I saw the Tropicana hotel - it was a big older pink building with a lot of people coming and going. There seemed to be a lot of low budget hotels on this side of the street. I guessed that this would most likely be where the street life part of the strip was.

I saw The Excalibur Hotel and Casino. The scenery started to change and there seemed to be more people. I saw the sign for The MGM and the golden lion and pulled in front to the valet. I was finally at my hotel and I wanted to hurry up and get checked in so I could check out the strip. I tipped the valet and walked through the big doors with lions on them into the lobby of The MGM Hotel. A sexy girl walked past and blew me a kiss as I approached the desk for check in. The lobby was full of people standing around talking. A group of people walked past loud and seemingly drunk. I stood in line and thought to myself about how much fun it was going to be to be in Vegas; single and with money to blow.

I stepped up to the desk and pulled out my driver's license and credit card. The girl at the desk was a short caramel colored girl who was so beautiful it was hard to figure out what her nationality was.

"Hello beautiful I have a reservation for Jason Gaines," I said smiling at the beautiful girl.

"Okay Mr. Gaines I have you in one of our Jacuzzi Suites," she said as she punched in the information from my license and credit card on her computer. A young guy wearing a bellman's uniform walked up behind me and put my bags onto his cart. When the clerk gave me my room key he showed me to the elevators. I pushed the button for the 18th floor and we were on our way.

The room was beautiful. White carpet and white furniture filled the room from wall to wall. The Jacuzzi was in a corner in the far side of the room and the balcony opened on the other end with a view over looking the strip. The bellman handed me a tourist brochure with ads for everything from food to escort services. Inside of the brochure the bellman had put his business card with an ad for girls at hourly rates.

"If you need anything at all just let me know! I'm the man with all the hook ups my brother," he said as I handed him a tip. He turned and left the room and I walked out to see the sun set over the city of sin.

The lights from the city were like nothing I had ever seen. It wasn't even all the way dark yet and already the lights were bright enough to be seen from outer space. I remembered looking out at the city in Hollywood and thinking of where Jersey and I would go to take a break. It was hard to believe that it had been three years since she was killed.

I went back into the room and opened my suitcase. I took out the drawing of us and put it on the bed. Next I pulled out the bottle of Grey Goose I had bought for us the night she died. I had promised myself that I wouldn't drink it until I made it to Vegas, now it was time to take that drink. After a couple of shots I got dressed to go see the casinos. I put a roll of bills in my pocket, checked myself in the mirror and then headed out to start my first night in Vegas.

I walked down a long dark hallway into the casino. The sound of machines hitting jackpots all over the casino made it seem like everybody was winning money. An old lady sitting at a slot machine put her money in and pushed a button and the machine came alive with lights and sirens. As I turned the corner heading towards the black jack table a beautiful girl walked up and linked her arm around mine.

"Hey baby why are you walking alone? I think I'm going to have to fix that. My name is Heather."

"Well hello Heather my name is Yellow," I said as I continued walking to the black jack table. A waitress came over and took my drink order and walked away. I sat at the table and bought my chips. At first I didn't want to bet too big. I wanted to get a feel for the table. The waitress came back with drinks for me and my self appointed escort.

My first bet won, I was dealt twenty-one and beat everybody at the table. The next few hands I either busted or broke even. I finished my drink and got up from the table. I wanted to see more of the casino, so I asked Heather to show me around. We walked around for a minute then stopped to watch a high stakes game of poker.

Heather pulled me closer and took my drink.

"If you want to see the best part of Vegas, let's go back to your room," she whispered in my ear. I looked at her and grinned. She was a busty white girl with long sexy legs. Her blond hair hung down around her neck, dangling just above her voluptuous breasts. She was definitely a great piece of eye candy, but I had already figured out her game plan.

"Baby I just got here, I won't be ready to see that part of Vegas until later on tonight," I whispered back to her. She smiled and handed me a business card with her picture on it.

"Just call me daddy. I'll be waiting," she said as she did her best to walk away with a strut to catch my attention. I shook my head laughing to myself. Jersey wouldn't have given up so easily if it had been her trying to catch a date.

Everything I saw in Vegas seemed to remind me of Jersey. She would've been in heaven here. She was pretty enough to work in the casinos or hotels, and street smart enough to be working every hustle possible on the strip. I walked around some more and had a few drinks then went to see what was happening on the strip.

Chapter 2

The Strip

The strip was like Hollywood on steroids. I walked out of the hotel and was stopped by a street performer dressed as Michael Jackson. He grabbed my arm and started doing the moon walk. He was singing "Bad" and motioning that I was bad. I laughed as I threw a dollar into a hat he had on the ground and kept walking.

It looked like New Years Eve on Time square. A group of women walked past wearing almost nothing. A pimp was behind them who gave me a flyer advertising women at $45 per hour or two women for $79. A man with a dog was dancing to music being played on a boom box as people walked past and dropped money into a coffee can that he had on the ground.

People stood around handing out cards and flyers advertising everything available in Vegas which mostly consisted of prostitutes or strip clubs. It almost seemed like sex was selling better than food. It was like the only thing anybody cared about was gambling and sex. Even the huge electronic billboards flashed pictures of prostitutes.

At the top of a large building trimmed in gold I saw the famous Mandalay Bay sign. I decided to go in and check it out. The lobby was done in all white marble with silver trim. The souvenir and clothing shops all looked extremely expensive. I walked into the casino. It was dark and there were more card tables here than back at the MGM. A girl wearing a white button down belly shirt and a short black mini skirt walked past carrying a tray of drinks. Her bright red lipstick gave her face a seductive look as she winked at me on her way past.

I stopped and watched people who were gathered around a roulette table. A man had placed a very large bet on black thirteen. The wheel spun and the ball rolled around and landed on black thirteen and the crowd went wild with cheers. He placed another bet this time on 26 red and lost. I walked away and stopped at a poker table.

I sat down and bought in. I had sat next to a pretty oriental lady who looked like she was doing very well in her night of gambling. The dealer dealt the cards and I almost lost it when I looked at my hand. I had been dealt three queens. When the dealer put the first card on the table I couldn't believe what I was seeing. I kept my cool and raised $100. The oriental woman raised to $300. At first I started to fold but decided to go all in at $1000. When I put my cards on the table I knew that there was a chance that she had a better hand than me and I started to sweat. She flipped her hand over and had a pair of aces. I had won. I decided to collect my winnings and move on.

Another pretty girl in the same black and white outfit as the first waitress I had seen came over and offered me a drink. I was already beginning to feel pretty tipsy but I took the drink anyway. It seemed like the drinks were getting stronger but it might have just been the fact that I had already been drinking before I left the room. I downed the drink and walked over to try my luck at the roulette table.

I lost the first three bets I placed and quickly figured out that it just wasn't my game. I walked away from the table and noticed a group of white girls looking at me smiling. I waved and walked up to another poker table. I was about to buy in when one of the white girls walked up and asked if I wanted to go with them to their room.

"I'm not looking to buy anything baby," I said as I motioned for the waitress for another drink.

"We're not selling anything, we just want the company of a sexy black man," she replied. I turned around and looked at her friends who were standing around a slot machine. The whole group was sexy. I couldn't believe my luck. I followed them out of the casino and through the lobby to the elevators. As soon as we were in the elevator one of the girls grabbed my crotch and started kissing my neck. One of the other girls turned around and reached in to feel my hard on too.

"I guess it is true what they say about black men," she said as she massaged my erection. I started to feel like a porn star. When the elevator got to their floor we all got off and walked to their room. The room was a luxury suite. It was huge.

The girl who had asked me to come up to the room walked over and pushed me onto the couch. She unbuckled my belt and unzipped my pants. I was ready. She pulled out my dick and started to kiss it then one of the other girls came over to watch. The other two girls were standing by the mini bar pouring us all drinks.

"Calm down girls, we all want to play with him," one of the girls standing by the mini bar said. The girl who had started giving me head looked up and laughed. She got up and sat down next to me on the couch.

"Have you ever been with a white woman?" she asked. I pulled up my pants and sat up looking at her with a grin.

"No, I haven't but it looks like that's about to change," I said as the other girl handed me a drink. I looked over at the girl still standing by the mini bar; she had dumped some cocaine on the mini bar and was separating lines with a credit card.

"Where are you pretty girls from?" I asked.

"We're from Idaho," the girl who had handed me the drink replied.

"Have any of you ever fucked a black man before?" I asked.

"There ain't many black men where we live. You're about to be a first for all of us," said the girl who had started to give me head. The girl who had been standing by the mini bar came over and held out a rolled up bill and motioned for me to do a line.

"Oh no, not me baby I'm not into going fast," I told her. I downed my drink and handed her the glass. "You can fill this back up though!" I said. The girls couldn't believe I had never tried cocaine before. I watched as they all did line after line. They kept trying to get me to try it and I continued to refuse. One of the girls started to unbutton her blouse. She opened her shirt and pulled her breasts out of her bra.

"If you want these you have to try the powder. No white girls if you don't try the white girl," she said as she put her breast back into her bra.

"Well I guess I better get going," I said. On the bed two of the other girls were kissing and undressing each other. One of them looked over at me.

"Just try it so we can all be on the same level," she said as the other girl started to kiss her body. I stood up and downed my drink. I walked over to the bed and sat my cup down.

"I guess I'll have to miss out," I said as I walked towards the door. I fixed my pants and reached for the door. The girl who had started to give me head walked up and kissed me on the cheek.

"If you change your mind come back, I wanted to finish the job," she said as she opened the door. I walked out and the door closed. I was really drunk now. I walked to the elevator thinking about what I had just done. Part of me wanted to go back to the room, but my better judgment made me get on the elevator. I needed some air. I had just missed out on having sex with four white women.

I left the hotel and went back out to check out the strip. I checked my watch. It was just after 10 o'clock and the strip was alive. Two mimes had a crowd gathered watching them perform. As I walked I noticed the large variety of prostitutes walking around. I laughed as I walked past a transvestite who looked like a clown from all of the make up he was wearing. I walked past an Elvis impersonator who was singing to a crowd of spectators.

A beautiful Hispanic girl walked up to me and asked for a cigarette. I gave her one and she put it in between her large breast. She wasn't dressed like a prostitute but I had a feeling she was. I almost wanted to take her back to my room and fuck the hell out of her but I kept walking. I needed a woman, the atmosphere made it hard to resist and I was just about ready to go back to the white girls. I reached into my pocket and pulled out the card that the bellman had given me. I looked at it but then I decided to see what I could get without having to pay for it. I walked into the Mandalay Bay to begin my hunt.

Chapter 3
Lisa, Lisa, Lisa

I walked back into the Mandalay Bay hotel feeling good. The air and the crazy crowd on the strip had given me a second wind. I walked past rows of slot machines filled with people placing bets and asked a security guard to tell me where the Red Square was. I was hungry and I had heard that they had the best steaks and martinis on the strip.

I sat at the bar and watched the bar tender make martinis and checked out the menu. I decided on the steak and lobster, and ordered a martini for starters. The room was lit with a calming red light. The crowd was a more sophisticated and laid back crowd than I had been seeing on the strip.

I saw a woman sitting alone at the other end of the bar who caught my attention. She looked to be in her early thirties, and she looked pretty classy. I imagined that she had to be a lawyer or some type of executive. She wore a black pants suit and her hair hung down around her neck.

She must've caught me staring because she smiled and raised her glass in my direction. I didn't want to seem too eager so I smiled back and then turned my attention back to the bar tender that had stacked a couple of glasses and was making more of the famous martinis.

When my food arrived I asked the bar tender to give her a drink on me. The steak was still sizzling, it was perfect. The lobster and asparagus were also a sight for sore eyes. I had almost forgotten about the pretty lady at the other end of the bar as I ate the first bites of my steak. It didn't even need steak sauce.

A few minutes later she came and sat next to me. I was just about done eating and had turned my attention to my Blackberry looking at my messages. She called the bar tender and ordered drinks for us and introduced herself. Her name was Lisa; she was from Chicago and was in Vegas on vacation. She said she was a prosecuting attorney, as I had guessed.

We talked and drank martinis getting to know each other for awhile then we walked out to the casino. She was tall and slim with a honey complexion. She was beautiful. She reminded me of Jada Pinkett in that movie with Jamie fox about the cab driver. I told her I had sold my barber shop and decided to take some time to myself away from the madness of California.

She said she had just gotten divorced and that she had come to Vegas to unwind and get her mind off of her ex. I had found the perfect woman to hang out with. I liked talking to her. She was educated, but still down to earth. We stopped at a poker table and watched a high stakes game. After that we went to the slot machines and talked some more as we fed the machines.

"Has anybody ever told you that you look like Snoop Dogg?" she asked with a smile.

"Yeah I've heard that before," I said. A waitress came over and took our drink order and walked away.

"Has anyone ever told you that you favor Jada Pinkett?" I asked. She laughed and continued to play the slot machine. All of a sudden her machine went crazy, she had won the jackpot. I laughed to myself thinking that she wasn't the only one who had hit the jackpot. I had found myself a treasure as well.

After we left the slot machines we decided to try our luck on the poker tables. I was feeling rather lucky so I started out betting big. In the first couple of hands I had lost pretty much everything I had won at the MGM. She wasn't doing too well either so we went back to the slot machines.

We had a few more drinks and played the slots for awhile then went for a walk on the strip. We decided to check out Fremont Street to see all of the street performers. We walked past a man spinning fire balls on chains while another man was juggling with burning bowling pins in front of The Four Aces casino. We watched for a second then continued walking.

A woman walked past wearing nothing but angel wings. Her body was painted with designs that covered her breasts, but the only item of clothes she was actually wearing was a pair of thong panties and high heels.

A contortionist folded himself into a box that didn't look like it could possibly fit him, while a girl played music on a violin. The violinist was playing a song by Alicia Keys: "*A*

Woman's Worth." We watched as she played, she was doing an excellent job. I dropped some money into a hat that was on the ground by her feet and we walked on.

As we were walking Lisa linked her arm around mine and pulled herself close. When we were halfway down the street she stopped and turned to face me.

"Let's go back to my room," She said as she looked into my eyes. I had been thinking of asking her back to my room but I had no problem going to hers.

"Okay, but do you want to have another drink first?" I asked.

"No, we can have drinks when we get there," she said as we started to walk. I knew what she had on her mind. She was ready to get it, and so was I.

As soon as we got to her room she grabbed me and started kissing me. I pushed her onto the bed and climbed on top of her kissing and undressing her. I unbuttoned her blouse and exposed her perfect round breasts. I slowly kissed her nipples while I unbuttoned and took off my own shirt. I kissed her body and slid her pants off then kissed her from her knees to her thighs. I reached into my pocket and took out a condom; she got on her hands and knees and started to massage my erection then put it into her mouth and slowly gave me head.

She put the condom on me and pulled me back on top of her. I slid inside of her and kissed her as I thrust into her harder and harder. I kissed her nipples massaged her clit with my thumb as I continued to take long slow strokes into her.

She rolled me over and climbed on top of me and rode me as she rubbed her breast and played with her nipples.

An hour later as I took her from behind, her body began to tremble. The sound of her moaning louder and louder made me explode inside of her. I lay down next to her, and she collapsed onto the bed smiling. I had to catch my breath. I put on a new condom and slid inside of her again. She had the kind of body that made me want to keep giving it to her until she couldn't take it anymore. After round three I collapse and fell asleep next to her. She had been better than I had expected.

The next morning when I woke up she ordered breakfast from room service. As we ate she told me that she wanted to spend the day poolside and asked if I would join her. I told her I needed to go back to my room and get myself together but that I would love to hang out by the pool for awhile.

Chapter 4

Cuzzo in Vegas

I walked out of the room feeling like a million bucks. I got onto the elevator and was checking myself in the mirror when the elevator doors opened. I couldn't believe my eyes. A beautiful girl dressed in a housekeeper uniform walked on to the elevator. I was almost sure that I knew her from somewhere. I didn't want to stare, but it was killing me. Then it hit me like a ton of bricks. I knew exactly who she was. It was my high school sweetheart, Dawn.

She didn't even notice me. It was definitely her though. I didn't even know what to say to her. The last day that I had seen her was when I had broken her heart way back in high school. The elevator stopped and she got off. I was sure it was her, the elevator doors closed and she was gone. I thought about all of the things that had happened to me as result of that break up. I wanted to try to see her again.

I left the hotel and went back down the strip to my room at the MGM. When I got to my room my message light was blinking. I looked at my cell phone and remembered it had been off all night. I turned it on and picked up the hotel phone to check my messages.

CLARK KENT

My cousin Smooth had been trying to get in touch with me all night. He was in Vegas and wanted to hook up with me. I called his phone and he answered on the first ring.

"What up Cuzzo! We here nigga. Where the fuck you been fool?" Smooth said when he answered the phone.

"You know me nigga, I been kickin it all night out this motherfucka fool. I'm at the room tho whats up?" I said as I sat on the bed.

"We'll meet you in the lobby in five. We got a room up in here too!" he said.

"What's up wit all that "we" Shit? Who you wit?" I asked.

"Nigga! I got Diamond and some mo bitches. I'm out here getting money. I ain't on vacation fool," he replied. I hung up the phone and hit the shower. It was going to be a fun night.

An hour later I called Smooth and met up with him in the lobby. Smooth was wearing a white Nike sweat suit with all white Air Force Ones, with a white Godfather hat and Ray ban glasses. I was wearing True Religion jeans, a white T-shirt, and Jordan's. We walked through the casino to find a bar.

We had been planning this trip for three years. Smooth had been coming to Vegas regularly, and had become a regular both on the strip and in town. When we got to the bar Smooth told me he had been working on a plan that would make us a lot of money. He knew about a big diamond heist that would be going down off of the strip.

A Russian mafia boss was going to be robbed by a Sicilian gang. The Sicilians needed us as a diversion because the Russians would immediately know that they had been set up by the Sicilians. We were the ones who would be delivering the diamonds to the Italians after the heist had gone down. The payoff for the delivery was $100,000 in cash.

"So why would they trust us to make the delivery?" I asked.

"Because no one would ever suspect two street thugs to be moving a million dollars worth of diamonds through Vegas in broad day light," he replied. We finished our drinks and went to the valet to pick up my rental car. We were going for a ride to see where it would all be going down. We pulled onto Las Vegas Boulevard. and headed towards Sunset. The house was on a desert plot about three miles from the strip. When we found the house we pulled into the dirt driveway and got out of the car.

The house looked abandoned, there was no sign of any activity anywhere around. A crow cawed from a fence post. I could hear the distinct sound of a rattle snake somewhere close. If this was where the heist was going to go down there was definitely no chance of there being any witnesses. My only question was why anyone would bring a million dollars worth of diamonds to such a deserted location in the first place.

CLARK KENT

The front door to the house opened and a big guy wearing a black suit walked onto the porch. He looked like a character from the Sopranos. He lit a cigar and motioned for us to follow him inside. Once we were inside I understood exactly why the heist was going to go down here. The inside of the house was totally opposite of the outside.

The house was furnished with lavish expensive furniture. Everything was state of the art. We followed him through a room that led to a stairway to the basement. The basement was full of TV screens that were used for simalcasting various sporting events. Tables were set up for poker games, and there was even a bar in the far corner.

A balding Italian man sat at a desk in another corner of the room reading a newspaper. He was wearing an expensive suit and had a gun with a silencer fitted to it on the desk. He folded the paper and stood up.

"Gentleman please, come in and have a seat. We have a lot to talk about," he said with a smile. We sat in the two chairs that were placed in front of the desk. The guy who had brought us into the house put four shot glasses on the desk and filled them with Scotch.

"How's my main brother from another mother?" he asked Smooth. Smooth stood up and shook his hand.

"Vinny! It's good to see you again. You still owe me from our last business venture," Smooth said as he picked up one of the shot glasses. Vinny reached into the inside pocket of his suit coat and pulled out a stack of money. He tossed it onto the desk and Smooth picked it up.

"I added a little something for the wait," Vinny said as he sat down and motioned for Smooth to do the same. "Is this the cousin you told me about?" he asked.

"This is my little cousin Ace. He's the only person I would trust to help me with our plan," Smooth said. We raised our glasses for a toast and downed the Scotch. Vinny told us the plan and where we were to take the diamonds once the heist was finished then he pointed the gun with silencer at us and told us that if we fucked up his plan he would kill us. He put the gun back on the desk and smiled looking at us.

"We will be in touch; in the meantime you and your cousin need to be seen spending money. I want you two to look like two guys just having a good time in Vegas. I added some spending money to the money I owed you Smooth. When it's time; one of my people will contact you. Until then don't come back here at all. You got that Smooth?" Vinny said as he stood up and nodded at the guy who had let us in. We were escorted back out of the house and headed back to our hotel.

Chapter 5

The Plan

We left Vinny's and went back to the hotel. I had been dying to get to the MGM buffet. I was starving. When we got inside I went straight to the crab legs and piled my plate. Next I went to the steak being grilled. The buffet was huge. They had everything you could think of. I ate like it was Thanksgiving dinner.

I told Smooth I would catch up with him in a few hours. I needed a nap. When I got to my room once again my message light was blinking. I picked up the hotel phone and checked the messages. Lisa had left a message saying I could find her by the pool at the Four Seasons. The next message blew my mind.

"Hello, this is Dawn. I saw you and thought I'd look you up and say hello. I hope you enjoy yourself here in Vegas." Her voice still had that soft sweet sound. I couldn't believe she had left a message. How in the world could she have even found out where I was staying? I wondered.

I hung up the phone and sat on the bed. I had so many things going on at once that it was beginning to get hard to remember which direction I was going. I rolled a blunt and poured a shot of Grey Goose. It was only my second day in Vegas and already I had a full plate.

CLARK KENT

I called Lisa and asked if she wanted to have a drink in the Jacuzzi in my room. She told me she would be right over. I had left an impression on little miss defense attorney. Twenty minutes later I opened the door and in walked the sexiest woman I had seen all day. Lisa walked in wearing a bikini top, and tight jeans. Her tall stilettos made her legs look long and sexy. I could tell from the way she was walking that she only had one thing on her mind.

I stripped off my clothes and got into the Jacuzzi and watched as she stripped out of hers. She walked to the Jacuzzi and got in. She sat on my lap and slid me inside of her. She had been waiting for this since I had left her this morning. When we were done the combination of the hot water and the steamy sex had me worn out. I lay on the bed next to Lisa. She was smiling with her eyes closed. I closed my eyes and drifted off to sleep

I dreamt that I was back at Forest Hills Park with Dawn. She was grown now and she still had her normal sweet demeanor, and her soft sweet voice. She was wearing her housekeeper uniform. I dreamt that she had told me there was something she needed to say to me. Every time I asked her what it was she turned her head away from me.

She had tears in her eyes and her body was trembling. Something was wrong but she wouldn't tell me what it was. The sky became dark with clouds, and I could hear thunder. The trees were suddenly bare and the sky was dark purple. When she turned around again her eyes were completely red and she looked like a demon. She opened her mouth and let out a howl so loud it hurt my ears.

I jumped awake and sat straight up on the bed. I looked around and found that it was dark and I was alone. How long had I been asleep? I wondered. I got up and picked up my phone. It was almost ten o'clock. I had slept for at least five hours

A note on the counter told me that Lisa was going back to her room to get ready for the evening. She wanted to hang out with me again. It seemed she was getting clingy. She had drawn a rose next to her name. I had to admit I had really been rocking her world and taking her mind off of her "ex" as she had put it.

I jumped into the shower to get dressed for the evening. I had to get fly for the evening it was definitely going to be a night to remember. Once I was dressed I called Smooth, who told me to meet him in the casino. I walked into the casino five minutes later ready to have one hell of a night.

When I walked up to the poker table Smooth was sitting at he was winning. Diamond stood on his right side and two other girls stood on his left. One of the girls on his left smiled and whispered into Smooth's ear. He looked up and smiled.

"Ace my nigga! It's about time yo ass showed up! Baby check this nigga out!" Diamond ran around the table and hugged me. She looked different than she had looked the last time I had seen her. She was still looking good but she looked like she had aged a bit since I had last seen her.

CLARK KENT

"Ace! How have you been? You know we wouldn't have missed this for the world bro," Diamond said as she grabbed my hand and led me around the table. "Meet my girls; Candy, and Monique. Girls, this is Smooth's cousin Ace," she said. The girls walked over to hug me and I couldn't believe my eyes. They were fine. One of the girls was light skinned with long hair and a curvy figure. The other girl was a blond with incredibly large breasts. She looked like the real life version of Jessica Rabbit.

Smooth stood up and gave me a hug. We walked away from the table and the girls followed us. When we came to a row of slot machines we stopped and sat down. Smooth put some money into the machine and looked around to make sure nobody was in earshot.

"Cuzzo, I got the word that the move is going down in two days." He said. He looked around again then said; "They got a UPS truck that we'll be driving. Once we get the diamonds we ditch the truck and roll out in your rental. We'll lay low and wait for the call and drop off the diamonds in Cali." My cousin Smooth was always thinking about money. If he did something it was never hard to figure out his motive: money.

Smooth didn't even like being in the casinos because he only saw them as a way to cause him to loose money. After five minutes at the slot machines Smooth got up and motioned for Diamond and the girls to follow us. We walked outside to the strip and Smooth nodded at Diamond and she took off walking with her girls.

I lit a cigarette and inhaled the smoke. Just that fast Smooth had thrown a guy to the ground and had his pistol in the guy's face. Apparently the dude had tried to pick pocket Smooth and Smooth had caught him. I pulled Smooth up off of the dude before a scene could be made.

Smooth kicked him in the ribs as he scurried away. I grabbed Smooth to calm him down and we walked back into the hotel. We took the elevator up to the 23rd floor where Smooth's room was. When we walked into the room I couldn't believe it. Smooth had rented a suite. It was bigger than some people's apartment.

The furniture was all black and the carpet was white. Plants and trees grew in planters set through out the room. It looked like something from a video. I expected to hear music start and see Snoop Dogg come out singing "Gin N Juice." Smooth disappeared into the room and left me standing in the front room. I sat down and began to roll a blunt.

Chapter 6
The Strip Clubs

Smooth came out of the room a few minutes later with shot glasses, and a bottle of Patron. He poured us shots and sat down in a chair across from me.

"Tonight nigga, we are about to kick it little cousin," Smooth said as he tossed a small zip lock bag containing two burgundy pills onto the table. "Tonight we're getting thizzed fool. Then we bout to go to the strip club and make it rain on some hoes!" he said as he downed his shot. I downed my shot and picked up the baggie.

"What the fuck is this nigga?" I asked as I dumped one of the pills into my hand.

"Nigga those are triple stack extasy pills. That shit is gonna have our asses on the level fool," he replied as he snatched the bag from me and flipped the other pill into his mouth. I wasn't used to seeing Smooth do any drugs other than weed. I figured if he was doing it couldn't be too bad. I put the pill in my mouth and swallowed it down with a shot of patron.

"So what's up Cuzzo? Where are we goin first?" I asked as I poured another shot.

"I figure we can start out at Sapphire. That's where the girls are workin tonight."

"I heard that Scores was the shit too. We gotta step off in there my nigga."

"Don't worry cuzzo by the end of the night you won't be mad no matter where we end up. We bout to kick it tonight," he said. I was starting to feel the buzz coming on from the pill. I was feeling that same almost out of body feeling I had felt the first time I smoked weed. I stood up and walked to the window to see the view.

Smooth came back into the room and we headed out. We got on the elevator and started going down. The elevator stopped on the 13th floor. The doors opened and four sexy prostitutes got on the elevator. Smooth started talking to them and kind of flirting. He told the girls we were headed to Sapphire and one of the girls laughed. She told him he was wasting his time and that he should call her and her girls. Smooth laughed at her and told her he had bitches working too.

When we reached the lobby Smooth didn't even let them walk off first. As soon as the doors opened he pushed past them and we went to pick up his car from the valet. We hopped in and rolled out on our way to the strip club.

As soon as we pulled up in front of the club one of the bouncers walked over and opened Smooth's door. Smooth got out and gave the bouncer some money and the bouncer signaled for the valet to park the car. Smooth already seemed to know everybody. When we walked inside they didn't even check us for weapons. The manager of the club walked up wearing a black suit with a white shirt and a red tie. He reached out and shook Smooth's hand and led us to the VIP area.

The club was dark, black lights shined from poles with lava lamps built into them. As we walked through the club I noticed the dancers checking us out. When we got upstairs to the VIP area a sexy oriental girl wearing neon green lingerie came up behind us carrying two bottles of expensive champagne. She sat the bottles on a table in front of us and opened them. Smooth grabbed one of the bottles and sat down with it like it was a forty ounce of beer.

Candy and Monique walked over and sat by Smooth. Candy whispered something in Smooth's ear and got up and walked away. Four more girls walked over and sat with us. A pretty girl who looked like she was fresh out of a college fantasy sat on my lap and introduced herself. Her name was Lexi. She had sexy round breasts and thick curvy legs. She wore a silver wig and silver glittery eye make up. She was definitely one of the sexiest girls I had seen in Vegas.

"Do you want this dance Daddy?" she asked as the DJ announced the next song.

"Yeah baby let me see what you working with," I replied. She started grinding her hips on me. It was like I could feel every part of her grinding on me. She spun around and dropped to the floor with her head in my lap. She put her mouth on my erection and it was like she was giving me head through my pants.

She slowly danced her way back up into my lap. She untied her top and wiggled her big sexy breasts in front of my face. Next she leaned in and blew into my ear. As she grinded her hips on me I could feel her pussy massaging my erection. She wrapped her arms around my neck and started doing circular motions with her waist on my lap. She kissed my cheek and turned around again this time sitting on my lap facing away from me.

She put her head down between her knees and started making her ass jiggle. The jiggling became more of a clapping motion with her ass cheeks. She was one hell of a lap dancer. She slapped her ass looking back at me as the song ended. She got up and picked up her top from the floor then sat back on my lap.

"How was it Daddy?" she asked. I looked at her smiling. The lap dance didn't leave much to the imagination about how good she would be in bed.

"That was pretty cool," I said with a smirk. I was really feeling the ectasy pill now. My senses were in over drive. I picked up my bottle and took a swig trying my best not to show how much I had really liked the lap dance. Diamond walked up with Candy and sat next to us.

"Hey brother! Are you havin fun?" Diamond said as she threw a phony smile at Lexi.

"You know me, I'm just chillin," I replied. Candy came over and sat on my lap.

"Daddy let me show you how this is done," she said as she started dancing doing her best to make Lexi look like an amateur. She was doing a really good job too. For the next five or so songs they were going back to back. I was in paradise. Smooth snapped his fingers and signaled for the girls to leave. They all got up and walked off.

"Let's make it rain on these hoes right quick!" he said as he stood up and walked to the railing overlooking the rest of the club. He pulled out two huge rolls of $1 bills. He handed me one and took the band off of his. He started throwing money over the railing. I took the band off of my money and did the same. The strippers were going crazy. We were balling.

Smooth called for the manager and told him to set us up a Patron bar. We sat back down and toasted with our champagne bottles. A waitress came up with a bottle of Patron on a tray with glasses, salt, and lemons. Diamond came back in with a different group of girls. All of them were top notch girls.

Diamond introduced the girls and we all started taking shots. An hour later we all left the club and rolled out in Smooth's car. We went to a club called Olympic Garden, then to another club called The Palomino Club. After going to all the clubs we were hungry so we went to eat at the Red Square. There were two of us with six girls and everybody was super drunk.

Chapter 7

Easy Money

When we got into the Red Square and got seated I got up to go to the restroom. As soon as I turned the corner I saw Lisa sitting alone at the bar. I walked over and sat beside her.

"Is this seat taken?" I asked as I sat down. She turned and looked at me and flashed a fake smile.

"I tried to call you. You were supposed to meet me by the pool, but I can see you were busy. It's okay though really I understand this is Vegas," she said as she held out her business card. "Call me if you ever need a good defense attorney!" she said as she got up and walked away. I got up and watched her leave. She was classy and probably too business like to have been my girl anyway, I thought to myself. I walked off and went to use the restroom.

When I came back to the table the waitress was putting our plates onto the table. Smooth was telling a story about how when we were kids I always got him into trouble. I laughed thinking of all of the trouble he had gotten me into. I sat down and enjoyed my steak and lobster tails. I looked at the business card that Lisa had given me. Her credentials were real - I had just missed out on a chance to finally have a woman who really had her self together.

We ordered martinis and finished our meals then headed back to Smooth's room with the girls. When we got to the room the girls all went straight to the Jacuzzi. Smooth turned on some music and we joined them. The girls had popped a bottle of champagne and were pouring glasses. Smooth got into the Jacuzzi with a bottle of Patron. The next thing I knew I was waking up in my own hotel room with three girls in my bed.

I didn't even remember coming back to my room so of course everything else was a blur. I was naked and so were the girls. I noticed that Candy was one of the girls. The other two I had no recollection of. I got up and walked to the bathroom. My head was throbbing. I splashed some water on my face and looked into the mirror.

My eyes were totally bloodshot and my face looked tired. I got into the shower and turned on the water as hot as I could stand it. The steam filled the bathroom as I began to wash up. The bathroom door opened and Candy walked in. She dropped her robe to the floor and got into the shower with me.

Candy was super sexy. She had a honey gold complexion with long straight hair. Her body was perfect and her attitude showed that she knew it. She had perfect firm breasts, and a sexy round ass. She was built like Jaylo before the ass reduction surgery.

After we were done in the shower we met up with Smooth and Diamond at the pool. We waited until the girls were in the pool then Smooth told me how we were going to get the diamonds. He told me that he had everything set up for the heist. We were going to show up dressed as UPS workers and rob the place. Afterwards all we had to do was lay low and wait for the call to deliver the diamonds.

It sounded easy enough, but I still wondered if it would really go down so smoothly. It seemed like that when dealing with Smooth there was always more to getting easy money than just getting money easily.

After Jersey died; Smooth had set us up to do an easy lick. He had told me that all I had to do was pick up Diamond from a hotel and bring her to him in Hollywood. It wasn't that simple.

When I pulled into the Hotel parking lot there were cops all over. As I pulled into the parking lot detectives were getting out of an unmarked car. One stood up and flashed his light in my face. I shielded myself from the light and found an empty parking space.

When I got out of the car I saw the detective coming in my direction. My first instinct was fear but I quickly turned it to innocence in the form of ignorance. I pretended to be oblivious to all of the commotion. I walked past him as if I didn't see that he was coming straight at me.

"Hey! Boy you better turn around and turn around slow! Keep your hands where the fuck I can see them! You hear me boy?" he said as soon he was in reaching distance. I stopped in my tracks. I was clean. I had no gun and no drugs on me. I put my hands up and stood still. Out of nowhere I felt the sting of a metal flashlight hitting me in the back of my head. I saw a bright light and then everything went blurry.

I woke up in the back of a squad car. My hands were cuffed behind my back. The car was moving fast and the two big detectives in the front of the car weren't saying a word.

"What the fuck man I didn't do shit! Why the fuck are y'all fuckin with me?" I said as I sat up. The detective in the front seat looked back at me with a mean look on his face.

"You know exactly why we're fuckin with you boy! We'll see how smart you are when we get to the station asshole!" he said just before he hawked up a loogie and spit on me in the back seat. The car jerked to a stop throwing my body against the back of the front seat. The back door opened and I was jerked out of the car by my shoulders.

I was thrown face down on the trunk of the car. The detective patted me down again then hurled me up and pushed me towards the entrance to the L.A. county sheriffs department. We walked into a set of doors that slammed closed behind us. The detective rang the intercom and the next set of doors opened.

I was taken into a room with windows for intake. My name and social security numbers were recorded, and then I was ordered to remove my jewelry and shoe laces. They took me through another set of doors and I came out into a bullpen. I still didn't even know why I had been arrested. All I knew was that Diamond had something going down at the hotel and I was getting paid to bring her back safely.

The bullpen was pretty crowded. There had obviously been quite a few arrests that night. I walked into the room and found a seat on a concrete bench. I saw a couple of guys looking at me but I wasn't worried about anybody messing with me. Everybody here shared a common enemy - the police who had arrested us.

Two minutes later two detectives came and pulled me out of the bullpen. It was very apparent that they weren't just pulling me out about an old parking ticket. They thought they had something and I was just about to find out what it was.

I was taken to a room with a desk and three chairs. A video camera was set up in the corner and the little red light was on. The detective sat me down in the chair behind the desk and uncuffed me. He sat down in the chair across from me and the other detective handed him a manila folder.

"Do you know why we're here Mister Gaines?" he said as he looked at me with a mean look on his face.

"No sir, I don't have a fuckin clue why we're here!" I said. He slammed his hands on the desk and leaned over the desk into my face.

"Do you like cutting up pretty little prostitutes? Did you think we wouldn't find you?" he yelled in my face. I didn't flinch. He sat down and opened the folder. My heart hit the floor as soon as I looked down. It was Jersey, her throat was stashed and her face had been beaten badly.

He flipped to the next picture and I threw up all over the desk. It was a picture of her from her neck down. Her body had been stabbed so many times that parts of her abdomen were missing. She had small puncture wounds all over her body like someone had stabbed her over and over with an ice pick.

The detective jumped back barely getting out of the way before the vomit hit the desk.

"You should be sick you sick bastard! You did this to her! You put that girl in a dumpster you fucking psycho!" he said as he grabbed the folder from the floor. I sat up and tried to focus but my eyes had filled with tears. I didn't want to see her like that. I couldn't stand the thought that it had happened to her like that.

I looked at the detective through crying eyes and told him I was innocent. I hadn't seen her since she had gotten into the car on Sunset. There was no way they could possibly pin this on me.

"We got video surveillance showing you and her together at the strip club approximately One hour before her death. One hour and twenty minutes later we see you and another male walking back to the car without her. Is there anything you would like to add to that?" said the detective who had brought in my files. He smiled then lit a cigarette. He blew the smoke into my face and laughed. "You're fucked little man. Why don't you just confess and get it over with."

Anger filled me and I almost wanted to scream, but instead I relaxed my face and took a deep breath.

"I want to speak to a motherfucking lawyer right now, bitches!" I said with a grin. The first detective cold cocked me and knocked me off of my chair.

"You're going down you nigger pimp piece of shit bastard!" he said as he lifted me from the floor and put me back in my seat. They walked out of the room and left me alone with the pictures of Jersey.

Chapter 8

Special Delivery

I was being charged with murdering Jersey. I was dressed in an orange jump suit and placed in general population. My bond was set at $500,000. Smooth and my aunt had gotten me a lawyer, but I still couldn't make bail.

A detective set up an interview with me and my lawyer. He was a balding white man in his early forties at best. My lawyer told me not to answer any question unless he told me to. I was brought into the interview room in handcuffs.

I sat down next to my lawyer and the detective sat across from us. He asked if I would agree to being taped, and my lawyer nodded that it was okay. He turned on a small recorder and sat it on the table.

"You're here because you are being charged with murder. I first would like to ask where you were on the night of October 6th?" My lawyer nodded and I told him that I was on Sunset in front of the strip club. I went through the story again and explained that I had gotten into it with somebody and hadn't seen the car she got into. The detective tried to trick me up but my lawyer stepped in and made him back off.

I was out of jail in a week. The charges were thrown out do to insufficient evidence.

CLARK KENT

When I got released Smooth was there to pick me up. He paid me the money that I was supposed to make for picking up Diamond and told me that the detectives had linked me to Jersey's murder because they had seen me with Diamond. Like I said there's no such thing as easy money when it came to Smooth.

So here I was once again caught up in one of Smooth's "easy money" schemes. When we got to Smooth's room he handed me a UPS uniform.

"Put this on nigga! We gotta work today," he said as he tossed me the brown UPS hat. I went into the bathroom and got changed. We had to send the girls to buy me shoes because all I had were Stacy Adams and Jordan's. Neither of which would look right in a UPS uniform.

The girls came back with a pair of all black Nikes. Smooth told me that we were going to make the delivery and be caught in a robbery. We were going to run out with the diamonds and the money as soon as the lights went out. I was nervous but ready.

We left the hotel and drove to the parking lot outside of Circus Circus. We parked the car and walked to a UPS truck that was parked near by. Smooth reached under the truck and came up with a set of keys. We got into the truck and took off.

We headed away from the strip to go to the house we had met Vinny at. As soon as we were onto the street, Smooth got pumped. He started talking about how after the heist was over he wanted to go on a cruise to Jamaica. He said he had already told Diamond that as soon as he had made the delivery that we were all packing our bags and going on a cruise.

"There you go wit that we shit cuzzo. Who is the "we" part of all this?" I asked.

"Nigga! Me, you, Diamond and Candy!" he replied. "I see the way you be lookin at that hoe nigga. You can have that bitch fool; I know you knocked the linin out of that muthafucka!"

"Whatever cuzzo! But I did tear that shit up tho!" I said with a laugh. We turned down a dirt street and Smooth stopped the truck.

"Okay let me go in first with the first box and you come in behind me. You got that? When the lights go out I'll get the diamonds while everybody is going crazy, and you just get back up the stairs and have that truck ready!" Smooth said with a serious look on his face.

"I got it cuzzo! Let's do this!" I said. Smooth put the truck in gear and we pulled off. We pulled in front of the drive way of the house we had met Vinny at. A black Lincoln Town Car was parked in the driveway along with two other cars that I couldn't see from the street. Smooth cut the truck off and climbed into the back of the truck. He ripped open a box and pulled out two Kevlar vests.

"Put this on under yo shirt nigga! Muthafucka's prolly gone start shootin in that bitch when the lights go off," he said. I stripped off my shirt and put on the vest. When we were ready we got out of the truck carrying two boxes. We walked up the driveway and onto the porch. Smooth knocked on the door and it was on.

The same big Italian guy as before opened the door. He led us through the house and down to the basement. In the basement Vinny was talking to two big Russian guys. One was standing and one was seated at the desk. Vinny looked surprised and motioned for us to bring the packages to him.

On the desk there was a cigar box lying open with a black velvet bag inside. The Russian reached over and closed the box as we approached. Smooth sat the box on the desk next to the cigar box and handed Vinny the clipboard. Vinny scribbled on the pad and handed it back to Smooth.

Just then the lights went out and the room became completely dark. I dropped my box and ran up the stairs. I heard shots start going off and then I saw Smooth emerge from the basement. More shots rang out as I ran across the steps and out into the yard. I ran as fast as I could to the truck and started it up.

Smooth ran out of the house carrying the cigar box. He jumped into the truck and we sped off. As we pulled away more gunshots hit the truck. We turned onto the next street and I floored it. I turned down another street and drove back in the opposite direction to make sure no one was chasing us. When I was satisfied that we had gotten away I slowed down and drove back to the strip.

We parked the truck back at the Circus Circus parking lot and drove back to the MGM in the rental. We had done it.

Somehow the heist had been successful. We had changed clothed in the truck and had put the uniforms in a bag. As soon as we were on the floor of the room I was staying in we put the bag into the garbage can.

We went into my room and finished off the Patron from the night before. All we had to do now was wait for the call. Smooth called Diamond and the girls and told them to come to my room. We rolled a blunt and smoked it while we waited on the girls. It had gone down better than planned.

We celebrated at the room for the rest of the day. We ordered our food from room service and we cleaned out the mini bar. Smooth and I talked about the cruise and going to Jamaica while we all drank champagne in the Jacuzzi. It was a night to celebrate.

When Candy found out that we were taking her too she lit up like a Christmas tree. We talked and kicked it for the whole night. Smooth had told her about Jersey and that I hadn't let a woman choose me since. She told me that she wanted to quit the life and go to school to be a lawyer. I laughed to myself because it seemed that every woman I had met lately had either wanted to be or already was a lawyer.

Chapter 9

Dusk Until Dawn

The next morning we got up and started packing. Smooth met with one of Vinny's people who gave him the key to a safe deposit box. He was told that the $100,000 and the instructions for delivery were in the safe deposit box and that he was not supposed to contact anyone until he was called on the phone they had given him.

Vinny had been shot in the shoulder and was in the hospital. The guy who had let us in and both Russians were dead. Smooth told us that the Russians would be sending reinforcements and looking for the diamonds. So far all anyone knew was that two black guys dressed as UPS workers had set them up and robbed them.

Vinny told his people that he had been robbed for a large amount of cash too. Both the Italians and the Russians were blaming each other. Vinny immediately put out the word that he had been set up by the Russians. Since neither of the two men who had come to him with the diamonds were alive to contest it, he also claimed that the diamonds were fake and only used as a prop to set up the robbery.

Smooth and Diamond went to their room to get there things. The instructions were simple. Take the diamonds to

CLARK KENT

Corona, California and wait for the call. I put the note back onto the table with the money. Candy continued to pack my things while she walked around the room singing.

"Woke up this morning... Smiled at the rising sun, three little birdies sat on my doorstop... Singing sweet songs, of melodies pure and true. Saying, this is my message to you ou ou! Don't worry, about a thing... Every little thing is gonna be alright"

I looked at the table again and at the cigar box. I couldn't believe it; we had just come up on a very good amount of money. I was definitely going to miss Vegas but I had no problem taking the money and running with it.

"Okay daddy we're all packed. I even took some of those soaps you liked so much," Candy said as she sat down in the chair next to mine. I poured shots of vodka and handed one to her. We made a toast to our new found friendship and we downed the shots.

Candy was a drinker. For every shot I drank she drank two. I looked at her and how happy she seemed. She was cool and she was definitely beautiful, but I wasn't really sure I wanted what she wanted.

I wasn't the kind of guy who went around trying to turn hoes into housewives. I understood the nature of their business and respected the boundaries. It was all business when I dealt with prostitutes. But Candy had that "fairy tales can come true" look in her eyes.

58

I wasn't sure why she saw me as the super hero that was here to save the day for her, but she did. I got up and went to look out of the window. I stared out at the city and wondered how to tell her that I didn't want her to change to be my girl. Actually I would rather that she continued to turn tricks and work in the strip clubs because that would give me the reason not to allow myself to have feelings for her.

"Baby, why do you want to get out of the life?" I asked. She sat her glass on the table and came to stand right by me. She grabbed my hand and looked me in my eyes.

"Daddy I never wanted to be in the life. Do you think a woman wants to spend her life being used by men? Do you even know what it feels like every time I turn a trick?

It's like I'm being paid to let men rape me... Every man has a different perverted thing they want to do to me... I have to get sodomized and beaten sometimes just to make a hundred dollars... And for what? So some other man can treat me like shit, talk down to me and take the money? Working in the clubs is no better. Being fondled is still the same thing as being raped.

They want to touch me in ways that make me uncomfortable so they can get a hard on, then they throw money at me and tell me to get out of their faces. I'm sick of being raped every day! That's why I want to get out of the life!" she said with tears in her eyes. She threw her arms around me and laid her head on my shoulder and started to cry.

CLARK KENT

I put my arms around her little waist and pulled her to me. I didn't even know what to say. I had never heard it put like that before. We stood in silence for awhile and then she went and lay on the bed. She was still crying. I was beginning to wonder if I even wanted to be in the life anymore.

I went to the bed and laid down next to her. Her body was amazing. She looked like the kind of girl you saw at the gym and fantasized about. Her hips were round and her ass was firm and tight. Her arms were toned but not too muscular. She looked like she could be in movies and not just the x- rated ones either.

She was abnormally beautiful. If I had met her in a different setting I would never have imagined her as a prostitute. She looked like she had come from a good home and had lived an easy life. At her age she should've been in college somewhere instead of selling her body in the streets.

I turned her over to face me and looked into her eyes. She had tears running down her face causing her make up to run. I wiped her tears away and kissed her on her cheek. She sniffled and grabbed my hands. I had to tell her what was on my mind. What had been eating me up inside for years and years.

"Baby, I understand what you're saying. I wish I was the kind of man who could settle down with a woman and allow myself to love or be loved. I wish I was even capable of loving. The truth is I'm afraid of love. I was in love once and I decided to let it go for selfish reasons, and I'm afraid of love's karma.

I'm afraid that if I allow myself to love someone; that one day my heart will be broken as karma for what I did to her. The funny thing is that I saw that same girl here in Vegas. I couldn't even build up the nerve to speak to her. Unless I make it up to her I don't feel that I will ever be able to love again."

I got up from the bed and walked to the window. I wasn't about to let myself tear up or show how weakened I really was. Candy came up behind me and grabbed me around my waist.

"Don't be afraid, daddy! I wont let love hurt you. You don't have to pretend to love me - all I ask is that you let me love you!"

Chapter 10

Run!

I looked at my watch. Smooth and Diamond had been gone for over an hour. I called their room but got no answer. I called their cell phones and still got no answer. I grabbed my bags and told Candy to grab hers and we went to the car to put our bags in the trunk.

We went back into the hotel and took the elevator to the floor Smooth's room was on. When the elevator doors opened all that I could see were security guards and policemen. Something terrible had happened and I was sure it had something to do with Smooth and Diamond. I got off of the elevator and Candy followed me down the hallway.

Half way down the hallway I could see that it was indeed Smooth's room that the police were coming from. I stopped a policeman and told him my cousin was the person who had rented the room. The officer escorted me to the doorway and called for a detective who was already in the room.

Through the madness I caught a glimpse of Diamond lying on the floor with two bullet holes in her forehead. The detective came out to the hallway and escorted me away from the room. He asked my name and my relation to the victims then asked when was the last time I had seen them.

CLARK KENT

I told him that they had left my room a little over an hour ago to collect their belongings and meet us at the check out desk. I told him that when I didn't hear back from them and that we came looking for them. The detective wrote down my statement and asked that we not leave the area until the investigation was complete.

He told me that a housekeeper had been in the room next door and heard shouting and then gunshots. She saw a tall black man and a tall white man running from the room. He said it appeared that they were ambushed by the men who were waiting in the room. They were both dead.

The officers brought us coffee and took down the information for contacting Smooth's mother. I told them that Diamond and Smooth had not been together long and that I didn't know the information for contacting her family. There was radio chatter and a few of the policemen and security guards had run for the stairwell.

The detective came over to us with three other policemen and escorted us to our car. We were told to follow the policemen to the police station; someone had just kicked in the door to my room and ransacked the room apparently looking for something. A housekeeper had been shot to death when she went in to clean the room.

The first thing I thought about was the fact that I was now carrying a million dollars worth of stolen diamonds and over $200,000 in cash. Everything was stashed in my bags in the trunk. I pulled into the police station parking lot and parked the car. When we got out I used the remote to lock the car and turned on the alarm. I wasn't sure they knew what kind of car I was driving but I knew they knew who I was.

The detectives took us into two separate interview rooms and started questioning us. It seemed like the lead detective knew that there was something I wasn't telling him. He asked the same questions at least four different times and four different ways to try to trip me up. I kept my story simple and told him that I had come to Vegas alone and met up with my cousin the morning after I had arrived. I told him that the girls had come from California with my cousin and that I had just hooked up with Candy. That part was true. When he asked about my whereabouts for the past three days I told him everything except the fact that we had ever left the strip. Video surveillance supported my alibis and Candy and I were released and freed to go after two hours of interrogation.

When we got into the car and pulled off Candy started crying. She was shaking and had a look on her face of pure horror. I understood how she felt but I had to drive as fast as I could and get as far away from Vegas as I could. I wanted to cry too but I couldn't let myself break down. I had to hold my composure and get us out of Vegas.

As I drove I continuously kept my eye on the rear view mirror to make sure we weren't being followed. I drove until I saw Russel Road and took a right. I drove until I saw signs for 15 South Las Vegas Freeway and tuned onto the freeway. I drove as fast as I could without being pulled over. The scenery quickly became all desert for as far as you could see.

I sped around two semis that were going too slow and switched lanes just in time to keep from slamming into a slow moving station wagon. I sped up and got to the front of the pack. I wasn't even thinking about the police anymore. I swerved through traffic switching lanes to pass more cars.

I switched lanes again just in time to merge onto 215 heading east. I ended up back on I-15 South. At first I wondered if I had made a wrong turn but I didn't want to stop to see. After a while I figured out that I was going in the right direction and kept up a good pace.

I drove for almost 3 hours until I saw the exit for Hidden Valley Parkway. I got off of the freeway and turned onto Hamner Avenue. I saw a sign for Fantastic Café and pulled into the restaurant parking lot.

When I turned off the car I looked over at Candy, who was fast asleep. She looked like a baby who had cried themselves to sleep. Her mascara had dripped down her cheek leaving tear tracks on her face. She still was beautiful though. I tapped her on her shoulder and woke her up.

She opened her eyes and yawned like a bear waking up from hibernation. She sat up and looked around.

"Where are we daddy?" she asked.

"Cali baby!" I replied.

"Damn! How long was I asleep?" she asked.

"I don't know baby I didn't even notice when you fell asleep. All I was thinking about was getting us the fuck out of there. Let's get something to eat baby. Come on," I said as I got out of the car. I locked the doors with the remote and turned on the alarm as we walked into the restaurant.

I ordered a burger and fries and Candy ordered a salad. While we were eating I asked her if there was somewhere I could drop her off until I made the delivery. I told her that I didn't want her to be there in case something bad went down. She told me that she had a house in Riverside not too far from where we were and that I could drop her off there.

"Promise you'll come back daddy!" she said with a pouty look on her face.

"Baby I don't make promises. I can only tell you that if everything goes right, I want you ready to go on that cruise with me." After we ate I let her drive and I took a nap. When we pulled up to her house I woke up. I got out of the car and got her bags from the trunk. I checked my bag and made sure that the cigar box and the money were still in place then I followed her up the driveway to the house.

Her house was nice. She opened the garage door and walked to the driver's side of a convertible Mustang and bent down looking under the car. She reached under the car and picked up a set of keys. When she came up she leaned against the car and started to cry.

She turned and walked into the house and I followed her in. The first thing I noticed was that there had been a struggle here. Broken dishes and various other things had been knocked off the counter. I looked into the dining room area and saw that the table had been turned over and a chair lay next to it broken.

"What the fuck happened here?" I asked. She looked like she was about to explode with anger. She was breathing hard and crying with a very angry look on her face. She stormed off running to a bedroom. When she came out of the room she was carrying a big automatic pistol. She pointed the gun at me, and started moving slowly in my direction.

"Did you know?" she asked as she picked up a pack of cigarettes from a shelf.

"Did I know? What the fuck is you talking bout and why the fuck is you pointing that pistol at me?" I said with my hands up. She lit the cigarette and blew the smoke out looking at me with an angry look.

"They killed my husband! They took my life from me! I wasn't in Vegas on no fuckin' vacation those motherfuckers came here and kidnapped me!" she said as she cocked back the hammer. My heart was beating so fast I thought it would give me a heart attack. "Did you know?" she yelled.

"I didn't even know they were going to Vegas. I was there for my own reasons. I thought you were just one of his girls!" I explained as I looked her into her eyes. She lowered the pistol and sat down on the couch.

"They said he owed Smooth a bunch of money… He had been selling dope for Smooth and he got robbed…The next thing we knew Smooth and his boys started coming around threatening us. Derek went to try to make a deal with Smooth and he never came back.

Two weeks later his body was found in Long Beach. He had been shot execution style and his naked body was found dumped in an alley. The police never found the people who killed him," she said as she stubbed out the cigarette. "After the funeral Smooth started coming around threatening me about dope money that Derek owed him. He said if I didn't come up with the money they were going to kill me too. I didn't know what to do.

My uncle flew out from Chicago and helped me sell the rest of the dope that Derek had left when he was killed. We paid Smooth the money and my uncle told him to stay away from me. At first he did, but as soon as my uncle left town Smooth started harassing me again.

I came home one day and he was sitting in my living room," she told me.

"Wow! I had no idea. I didn't even know about the heist until I saw y'all at the casino," I said. She tossed me a cigarette and a lighter.

"Are you going to come back?" she asked as she uncocked the pistol and took out the clip. I looked at her and stood up.

"Yeah baby I'll roll back through when I'm done," I said as I walked back to the kitchen. I opened the refrigerator looking for something to drink and found beer. It was ice cold. After what I had just heard I was going to need a drink. I walked back into the dining room and turned over the table. "Damn baby... I'm sorry you had to go through that bullshit. I didn't even know Smooth was like that," I said as I turned over a chair and sat at the table.

"I knew when I met you that you didn't know. When you took me back to your hotel room I started to run... But I felt safe with you! I was afraid of what would happen to me if I wasn't with you," she said as she came and stood beside me. "What time do you gotta make the drop off?" she asked. I stood up and looked out at the car. I had forgotten about the phone.

I ran out to the car to get the phone out of the trunk. When I went to check for missed calls I noticed that the phone had been off. I turned it on and walked back inside. I told Candy that I needed to wait for the call and that I was going to stay at her house until I got it.

After waiting for a couple of hours and still not getting a call I decided to have Candy take me to return the rental car and drop me off at my room. She had cleaned up her house, took a shower and changed clothes. She was wearing tight jeans and a Prada blouse. Her hair was combed back into a pony tail and she looked like Gabrielle Union.

When I asked her if she would take me she ran and jumped in my arms.

"I get to see where you stay? Does that mean I'm special or something?" she said with her arms around my neck hugging me and looking in my eyes.

"Let's just be cool and keep the titles off of things. But yeah it means you might be a little special," I told her. We left the house and she followed me in her Mustang to drop off the rental car.

Chapter 11

Run Faster!

When we got back to my room she pushed me against the wall and started kissing me. We undressed each other and laid on the bed. After nearly an hour of sensual steamy sex she told me she needed to go. I told her I would call her as soon as I was done with the delivery and walked her to her car.

On the way to her car I showed her my Cadillac that had been parked in the garage while I was out of town and told her that we would have to swap cars some day. She laughed and told me she wouldn't mind driving my car if I promised not to get any speeding tickets in hers. I laughed and then walked her to her car. I needed a drink and a nap. I was tired.

I went back to my room and took a couple of shots. I passed out and fell into a comfortable dream.

The sound of someone jiggling the door handle woke me up. I sat up straight and listened to be sure, but I had definitely heard someone jiggle the handle to my hotel room. I was almost sure no one knew I was here, and I was even surer that no one here knew I who I was. I had always been low key around this area. Then I heard it again. I got up and tip toed to the door to look through the peep hole.

It was a tall dark skinned man in a dark suit wearing gloves. I tip toed to the window to see if I saw anyone in front of the hotel. It had to be close to three in the morning.

There wasn't even traffic on the street. A black Lincoln Town Car with tinted windows was parked at the curb, and I could tell from the smoke coming out of the tail pipe that it was running.

The sound of someone knocking on the door made me turn around and creep back to the door. I looked through the peep hole and saw the same guy now standing with a gun in his hand. He knocked again, this time louder than the first time. I stood there frozen in fear wondering what to do. My heart was beating so hard that I thought it could be heard from outside of the apartment.

Then I heard the sound of footsteps in the hallway as if someone was leaving the building. I looked back out of the peep hole to see if he was still there. He was gone. I hurried back to the window and waited to see if he returned to the car. When he walked out of the building he walked to the car and the back window rolled down.

The man in the back seat of the car was white. The black guy leaned over and was talking to the guy in the back seat. While he was talking he pointed at my window. I had the curtains closed so I knew they hadn't seen me, but I wondered if they knew I was in the apartment.

The window rolled up and the car door opened. The white guy got out of the car and they walked back towards the building. I ran to the Lazy boy I had been laying on and grabbed my shoes. My coat was on floor, and my keys were in the pocket. I swooped up the coat and ran to the bathroom.

I put my shoes and coat on and opened the window. There was a ledge under the window that I could stand on to jump onto the roof of the garage. The room was on the third floor and it was my only way out.

I climbed out of the window and closed it, then stood off to the side of the window and listened to see if they would kick the door in. I had put the chain on the door before I went to sleep, so the only way they could get into the room was to kick the door in.

I heard the sound of someone knocking at the door, and waited to hear the door crash in. They knocked again, and banged on the door after not getting an answer. I waited but heard nothing more.

After about five minutes I climbed back into the window and crept to the door. I looked out of the peep hole but didn't see anyone. I walked to the window and looked out. The car was gone. I wondered if there was anybody in the hallway, but I was too afraid too look. I went back to the window and looked out again. There was no one outside. I walked back to the bed, and sat down. It was them, it had to be but how had they found me?

I opened my phone and looked at the time; it was 3:45am. I walked back to the door and looked out of the peep hole again. I didn't see anyone but that didn't mean there was no one waiting in the hallway. I sat back on the bed and tried to calm myself down.

The phone rang and I looked at the screen. The call was from a private number. I hit the answer button and listened. The voice on the other end sounded Russian.

"Where are my diamonds?" the person on the other end of the phone said. I told him that I had the info for the drop off and was ready to meet him at the specified drop off spot.

"Do you know who this is you ass hole?" the voice said. "I lost two very good soldiers when you fucking niggers robbed that house! I want my fucking diamonds!" I hung up the phone and sat there confused for a second. I was expecting a call from the Italians who had set up the heist in the first place, not the Russians who had been set up. I sat the phone back on the bed. No sooner than I had set the phone down it started to ring again. That told me that it was not a case of someone knocking at the wrong door in the middle of the night. They had found me.

I had to leave before they came back. I thought about the fact that there was only one way out of the apartment which was not really a good thing considering the fact that someone could be waiting in the hallway or in front of the building so I decided to go out through the bathroom window.

I grabbed my phone and the bag that I had brought with me to the apartment, and jumped out of the bathroom window. My car was parked in the garage and I was able to get to it without being seen. I put the bag in the trunk and walked down the driveway to see if there was anybody watching the hotel.

When I peeked around the corner of the building I saw the Lincoln parked at the end of the street. Driving out of the building was out of the question. They would definitely see the car pulling out onto the street and I would be caught.

I walked back to the car and made sure it was locked then I climbed the wall and jumped into the yard of the building next door. I walked to the back of the yard and followed a path that led to an alley. I looked out into the alley to make sure I wasn't seen then started walking down the dark alley staying in the shadows to avoid detection.

I came to a street and walked across to the alley on the other side. As I made it into the alley and ducked into the shadows I saw the Lincoln turn into the alley I had just come from.

They must've finally kicked in the door and found out I had gone out of the bathroom window. I had to find somewhere to hide because I knew they would be coming to this side of the alley when they didn't see me in the other alley. Half way down the alley I found a door on a building open that led to a stairway.

I went in and closed the door behind myself. I climbed the stairs two at a time and went to the roof of the building. I crossed the roof top to look down on the alley just as the Lincoln turned into the alley. It drove down the alley past the building and turned onto the street on the other side.

CLARK KENT

I needed a plan. I walked to the other side of the roof top to look out at the street. The Lincoln was driving slowly back in the direction of my hotel. I ducked down to make sure I couldn't be seen. I watched as the Lincoln stopped at the intersection at the corner of the street.

The Lincoln crossed the intersection and parked at the corner. They were watching my hotel room. My phone rang again and the caller I.D. read private again. I hit the talk button but didn't say anything.

"You're a dead man!" said a voice through the phone. I hung up and looked to see if the Lincoln was still in the same place. It was gone. Two minutes later it appeared, driving slowly past my hotel. Soon it would be daylight and the streets would be full of people going to work, and starting their day. If I waited I would be able to get my car out into the morning traffic and get away.

I sat down and pulled out the pack of cigarettes from my inside pocket. I took one out and held it for a minute staring at it. I had told myself I was going to quit, but that would have to wait now. I lit the cigarette and took a long pull. The mint taste of the menthol reminded me of York peppermint patties. I looked at my phone to check the time; it was 4:40am. I looked back down and saw that the Lincoln was still parked at the corner.

An hour later the sun had begun to rise and the traffic had picked up. I walked down the stairs through the building to the front door. A few people were walking up and down the street so I decided to go back out through the back door. I walked down the alley heading in the opposite direction of my hotel. When I came to the street I crossed and walked through the intersection.

A store was opening and a newspaper truck was parked in front of it. I walked across the street to the store and went inside. I bought a newspaper and went out to sit at the bus stop in front of the store.

I sat at the bus stop and pretended to wait for the bus. I had a clear view of the Lincoln at the corner; they were definitely watching my hotel. The car had Arizona license plates, which told me it was definitely the same people who had been chasing me. I remembered seeing Arizona plates on the Lincoln at Vinny's place.

I thought for a second and came up with a plan. I pulled out my cell phone and dialed 911. I told the operator that there was a Black Lincoln town car parked at the corner trying to lure young girls into the car.

Five minutes later two police cars pulled up behind the Lincoln. As soon as I saw the police pull up behind the Lincoln I ran back to the garage to get my car. I pulled out of the garage and turned onto the street heading in the opposite direction of the Lincoln.

I looked in my rear view mirror and saw that the police were still talking to the driver of the Lincoln. I had gotten away, but I knew it was only a matter of time before they found me again.

CLARK KENT

I drove as fast as I could without being pulled over. I stopped at a Shell gas station to fill up then got on the freeway. As I drove, I kept a constant watch of the road behind me making sure I hadn't been followed. I knew they would be coming after me. The only question was how long it would take for them to find me again.

I took an exit that had signs for a motel. I drove into the Motel 6 and looked for a place to park my car where it wouldn't be seen. I found a parking space behind the hotel beside a garbage dumpster. I locked the car and went to the office to rent a room.

The clerk was an Indian woman who looked to be at least fifty years old. I asked for a room where I could see the parking lot, and tipped her an extra hundred dollars to call my room if anyone came in asking about me. I told her that I was an actor and that I didn't want anyone to know I where I was staying.

The room was perfect. It was right above the office with a clear view of the entrance to the parking lot. If anyone pulled in I would see them before they ever had a chance to come looking for me.

The bathroom window faced the back of the hotel. It was big enough for me to climb out if I had to leave in a hurry, and my car was directly below it. I went to the car to get my bag and took it to the room. When I got back to the room I locked the door and took the cigar box out of the bag and laid it on the bed. The diamonds were still in the box along with the money. I poured the diamonds out of the bag and stared as they glistened from the light of the bed side lamp. They were beautiful. There had to be at least a hundred of them, each one was the size of a raisin.

I put them back into the black velvet bag and placed them back into the cigar box. It was the first time that I had been able to take a look at them. All I knew was that I was supposed to be taking them to a mob boss in Corona.

I had the phone and had checked it from time to make sure I hadn't missed a call. I knew that somehow the Russians knew about the phone, and probably knew I was supposed to be waiting for a call from the Italians.

I hid the box in a ceiling tile in the bathroom then I sat on the bed and turned on the television. It was almost noon and I wanted to catch the news. I needed to find out if the heist had made headlines.

Chapter 12
Mikey and Ivan

Mikey and Ivan were step brothers. Their mother was a black woman who had died giving birth to Ivan. Mikey's real father was a black man who had been killed in Vietnam. His mother had married Ivan's father when he was a baby.

Ivan was the smarter of the two, even though he was the younger brother. His father was Ivan Senior, a Russian immigrant and head of the Russian mafia in Reno. The two of them were total opposites. Mikey was dark skinned and Ivan didn't look black at all.

They had been given the job of finding the diamond thief and bringing both the thief and the diamonds back to Reno. They had been tracking the thief through a program that was able to hack into the GPS system of the phone being used by the thief.

If his dumb ass brother had listened and just kicked in the door like he had told him they would be back at home already. Instead they were being harassed by the police.

When the police pulled up behind their car Ivan had unplugged the power cord to the lap top and lost the signal of the satellite. He closed the lap top just before the officer had gotten to his window.

CLARK KENT

"Hello officer, how can I help you?" he asked. The officer didn't seem to be the friendly type.

"Put your hands where I can see them and step the fuck out of the vehicle!" the officer screamed as he snatched the door open. He was a young white police officer with a serious attitude.

Ivan threw his hands up and tried to look to see the cop. Mikey opened the passenger side door and was almost out of the car when the officer who had been standing behind the car shot him with a taser gun. He twitched and fell to the ground.

The officer at the driver's side snatched Ivan out of the car and threw him on the ground. They were searched and put into the back of the police cruiser. An ambulance arrived and Mikey was pulled out of the car and taken to the ambulance, while the police ran their names and checked for warrants.

The police searched the car and found two nine millimeter pistols in the glove box. Both guns came back registered. Mikey was tended to by the paramedics while Ivan was interrogated. The police said they were called about someone trying to lure young girls into a Lincoln town car that matched the description of the car they were driving.

When the police were interrogating Ivan, he had watched the diamond thief drive away. It was going to take another couple of hours to trace the phone again. On top of that he had to deal with his brother crying about being racial profiled.

After nearly an hour of interrogation the police let them go. Ivan needed a drink, and he needed one fast. He drove to the nearest bar and parked the car.

"Damn it Mikey! We had the son of a bitch! All you had to do was kick in the door!" Ivan said as he got out of the car.

"Bullshit! What if it was the wrong door? And who's to say he wasn't sitting there ready to blow my head off as soon as I kicked in the door?" Mikey said as he walked up behind Ivan.

They walked into the bar and sat at a booth. It was early and the bar had just opened. Mikey ordered a double shot of brandy, and Ivan ordered vodka. Ivan opened the lap top and began trying to hack the GPS system again. With any luck the thief was still in the area.

The problem with tracking the thief through the GPS system was that it could only give a rough estimate of where he was. When they had found it earlier all they knew was that the thief was in the hotel. They had been watching the hotel for hours and took a lucky guess as to which room the thief was in.

Ivan's cell phone vibrated in his pocket and he knew it was his father. He answered the phone and told his father what had happened. His father threatened to have someone else find the thief, but Ivan assured him that they would have everything taken care of within the hour. It was a lie and Ivan knew it as he hung up the phone.

"What did he say?" Mikey asked as he finished his drink.

"He said to tell you not to second guess me again moron," Ivan said.

"Bullshit! Why didn't you kick in the door if you thought you were so right?" Mikey replied.

"Because it's my job to find him and your job to catch him," Ivan said as he signaled for the waitress. They ordered burgers and two more drinks while Ivan tried to hack the GPS system again. After they ate and finished their drinks they paid the tab and left.

Chapter 13
Track Me If You Can

There was nothing on the news about the heist. As I was flipping through the channels I saw something that caught my attention. There was a movie on where people were tracking other people's whereabouts by using the GPS of cell phones. I thought about the men who were chasing me and wondered if they were doing the same thing to me.

I picked up my cell phone to check the GPS settings. Sure enough my phone was set to show my location. I changed the settings so that only 911 could track my phone's location then I took the battery out of the phone and put it in my pocket.

If they found me now it would have to be because they tracked me before I had figured out about the GPS system. I could also use my phone to throw them off by turning it on and leaving it somewhere. Now I had the advantage.

I went to the window and looked out. There was no sign of the Lincoln, or anything else that looked suspicious. I decided to go find some place to eat and figure out how I was going to make the delivery without the Russians catching me. Before I left the room I took the cigar box from the ceiling tile and looked for another place to hide the diamonds.

CLARK KENT

I looked around the room and decided to hide them in the light fixture over the bathroom sink. I turned on the light to make sure they couldn't be seen, and decided that it was the perfect hiding place. I put the cigar box with the money back in the ceiling tile and headed out to eat.

I found a sports bar not too far from the hotel. I parked the car and went inside to eat. The Sports bar was crowded with people watching the Lakers game. I found a table in the back and ordered a beer and some hot wings.

From my place in the back of the sports bar I had a good view of both the door and the parking lot. I thought about using my vantage point to test my theory about the GPS system. If I played it right I could lure the Russians to this location and sabotage the car they were driving when they came inside.

The Lakers were playing the Cleveland Cavaliers, and Kobe was on fire. The score was 88 to 74 and it was the third quarter. Kevin Love passed the ball to Lebron James who did a 360 slam dunk. The crowd went wild. The Lakers brought the ball back down court and Kyrie Irving stole the ball and threw an alley oop to Lebron.

It was an intense game and the Cavaliers were coming back. It was like they had been waiting until the end of the game to come alive. A foul late in the third quarter caused Kobe to be ejected from the game. By the end of the quarter the score was tied at 98.

I finished my hot wings and decided it was time to see if the phone was how I was being found. First I needed to make sure my car was hidden. I walked out to the parking lot and looked around for a second to see where I could put my car.

The parking lot was full but it still wasn't a good idea to park the car there, it would be too easy for them to spot it. Across the street from the sports bar was a used car lot. I thought about the fact that they knew what kind of car I was driving and decided to trade it in.

I pulled into the used car lot and parked next to a trailer that served as an office. A balding older man in a shirt and tie came out as I was getting out of the car .He hurried over to shake my hand and ask me if I was interested in buying a car. I looked around to see if I could find something I liked that was low key.

"I need something kind of plain looking that won't attract too much attention," I said as I looked around the lot.

"How about this Magnum station wagon? It has low mileage and because of the color and tinted windows it definitely won't attract much attention. You'll look like a soccer mom," he said as we walked over to the line of cars parked at the front of the lot. I looked at and asked how much he wanted for it. He told me it was selling for $5500. I pointed at my Cadillac and asked what he could do for me on a trade in.

The Cadillac was in excellent condition. He looked at it and told me he could give me $4000 for the Cadillac. I haggled with him for a few minutes and talked him into giving me $5000. We went inside to take care of the paperwork. I drove off the lot in the Magnum and parked it in front of the sports bar.

I looked at my watch, it was 3:00pm and I still hadn't got the call from the contact about the diamonds.. I pulled out my cell phone and turned it on. Almost as soon as it came on the phone began to ring. I answered it and didn't say anything. A voice with an Italian accent spoke in a quiet voice.

"At 6:45 in Riverside there's going to be a guy named Guido parked on the corner of Maryhellen Street by the park. He'll be waiting to hear about your trip," he said and then hung up the phone. I turned the phone back off and sat it on the bar and thought about how I was going to sabotage the Russians car when they came.

I ordered a beer and some more of the hot wings. The bar wasn't as crowded as it had been when I first came in earlier. The Lakers had lost the game and a lot of the people had left. It would be too easy for them to spot me if they came into the sports bar so I decided that I would have to put the cell phone outside in a bush or something. I finished my beer and wings and went back out to the parking lot to find a place to stash the phone.

The parking lot didn't really have many if any places at all to hide the phone where it wouldn't be easily found. There really wasn't any shrubbery that would serve as a good hiding place. The landscapers had done an exceptional job of keeping the trees and bushes perfectly trimmed. The sports bar was in a small strip mall that also housed a grocery store, a pawn shop, and a book store. Most of the land was parking lot.

I walked through the strip mall looking for a place to stash the phone, but found nowhere that the phone wouldn't be easily discovered by some random passer by. I thought about putting it in a garbage can, but decided that it would be just my luck that someone would come by and change the garbage can lining before the Russians could trace the phone. I needed to find somewhere else to stash the phone. The strip mall would not work for my plan.

I checked my watch and it was 3:45, I still had plenty of time to find a way to stall the Russians, and still make the delivery on time. I walked back to the Magnum and headed back to the motel. While I drove I continued to look for a place where I could stash the phone and still be able to lure the Russians without being caught.

Chapter 14

Blame

Ivan was a computer genius. He knew more ways to hack into computers than he knew people. He opened up the laptop as soon as he got into the car and started typing. Mikey stood outside of the car smoking a cigarette. They were total opposites. For Ivan it was always all business, but Mikey had a span of attention that would make a two year old look focused. Two girls walked by wearing Daisy Dukes and bikini tops. He winked at them as he exhaled a cloud of smoke.

"Hey! Bonehead hurry up I got him!" Ivan yelled from inside the car. Mikey waved at the girls and pretended not to hear him. Ivan opened the door and yelled again and this time he was able to get Mikey out of his female induced daze. Mikey turned and started walking to the car still looking over his shoulder. They got back into the car and pulled off.

Ivan opened the laptop again to check the location. He typed in the codes to get back into the GPS system but couldn't get a trace on the thief's phone. He pulled into a gas station and parked at the pump.

"Fuck! Fuck! Fuck! Fuck!!" Ivan yelled as he punched the roof of the car.

"What? What is it?" Mikey asked as he turned into a gas station.

"The fucking signal is gone! We lost it because you were too fucking busy looking at those bitches!" he said as Mikey walked into the gas station. He slammed the laptop closed and punched the roof again. Mikey walked back out of the gas station with a six pack of Coors light and a pack of Marlboro reds.

"What?" he said as he got into the car.

"We fucking lost him you idiot!" Ivan yelled.

"Well try again, we have a deadline remember!" He opened the door to get out just as Ivan swung and punched him in the face. Mikey snatched away and got out of the car. "Fuck you man! You're not blaming this shit on me!" he said as he walked towards the gas station. He looked back at Ivan with an angry look on his face and gave him the finger. He reached for the door but turned around and walked back to the car and snatched Ivan out of the car. He grabbed him by the collar and threw him up against the car.

"You don't think I remember how people treated me back in Moscow? You don't think I see how you and Dad look at me? How you both can't wait to blame it on the black fuckin' charity case that you all took in! My Mama was a dope head! She died of an overdose to get away from me. And now you and Dad want to blame me for every fucked up thing that happens! Fuck you man! Go to hell!" Mikey said as he let go of Ivan and started walking away.

Ivan didn't know what to say. He watched as his brother walked away and a tear dropped from his eye. Mikey was right. He did feel that way about him. If their father hadn't left and gone to the USA everything would've been different. His friends wouldn't have teased him for having a nigger brother.

Ivan got into the car and drove off to pick up his brother. At first Mikey wouldn't get into the car but after a few minutes he got back into the car and they drove off. Ivan pulled up the map again and typed in the last location they had gotten a hit on the phone. It was in Riverside close to Downtown.

They got on the freeway and went in the direction of the location. At first they rode in silence and after awhile Mikey decided it was time for a talk.

"How come you always blame all of your fuck ups on me?" he asked. Ivan didn't respond. As they drove on Mikey began to get angrier and angrier.

"You were the one who was too busy looking at those bimbos to come when I called you. It was your fucking fault!" Ivan said after letting an awkward silence linger.

"You lost the signal! You would've still lost the signal even if I had hurried to the car. Grow up and take some responsibility sometime asshole!" Mikey said as they pulled off of the highway at the exit for Riverside.

Chapter 15

The Set Up

I pulled into the hotel parking lot and parked the car. I went to the room to get the cigar box and the money. I took the bag out of the light cover and removed the ceiling tile to get the money from the cigar box. I put the money in one pants pocket and the diamonds in the other one. I decided to put the phone into the cigar box and leave it on the bed.

I ordered a pizza and waited. I figured it would take them some time to find my location again. I dialed the number of the Italian who had called me back and told him where I was and that I was being followed by someone in a black Lincoln.

I told them that I was hiding out in the room and wouldn't leave until somebody came and took the diamonds off of my hands. Forty-five minutes later the pizza arrived. I looked out at the parking lot and still didn't see any one out there so I decided to take the pizza and wait in the car.

When I got back to the parking lot I moved my car to the far end of the parking lot. I figured that I would have a clear view of the Russians when they came looking for me.

I waited in the car for almost an hour. I was just about to leave when I saw a black Lincoln town car pull into the lot.

The car parked by the office of the hotel and the same big black guy who had been at my door at the other hotel got out.

He went into the office and I saw the Indian woman show up at the desk. He looked like he was asking if she had seen me because I could see her shaking her head, telling him no. He walked back out to the car and said something to the driver. The Indian lady picked up the phone and appeared to be calling the room to give me the heads up. The driver pulled the car into a parking space and got out. They went up the stairs and stood at the door to my hotel room.

Another black Lincoln pulled in and parked. Four huge Italians who looked like hit men got out of the car. They looked up at the Russians standing at my door and one of the Italians pulled out a gun and started shooting at the Russians. The Russians tried to duck for cover but there was none.

The black guy kicked in the door and they dove inside. It looked like he had been shot. The Italians run up the stairs to the room and gun fire erupted from the window of the hotel. One of the Italians was hit and he went down on the landing. More gun fire came from the room and the Italians returned fire.

The Italian who had gone down was crawling towards the door. He pushed the door open and unloaded his gun into the room. The gun fire stopped and the Italians went into the room. I put the Magnum in gear and drove off before anybody had a chance to see me. I had just gotten away with the diamonds and the money.

I drove back to Riverside and pulled into Candy's driveway. At first I thought about just telling her that the delivery had gone down smoothly, but I decided to tell her what had happened. As soon as I knocked on the door she opened it and jumped into my arms.

"Oh thank God you're okay! I thought you were dead," she said.

"What are you talking about?" I asked.

"The news showed footage of the shoot out at the Motel 6! They identified you as one of the men who got shot," she replied. I couldn't believe it. How could they have thought I was one of the people dead? I had left the room over an hour before everybody arrived.

I walked into the house and sat on the couch. Her house looked a lot better than when I had first walked in. She had cleaned up and gotten rid of the broken chair. She came and sat next to me and turned on the TV.

At first there was nothing on the news about it, but then a late breaking report said that I was being looked for in connection to the shoot out. The reporter said that new evidence found that I was not among the dead. The police were not revealing any of the names of the people dead at this point in the investigation. A blurry image of me leaving the room flashed across the TV screen. Police were asking anyone who could identify me to call the crime stoppers tip line.

Candy turned off the TV and came to sit beside me.

"What happened?" she asked.

"They were tracking the cell phone. I came up with a plan to have the Russians and the Italians show up at the same place at the same time. I called the contact and told him I was being followed and that I would not come out of the room until somebody came and picked up the diamonds.

It couldn't have worked better. They all showed up at damn near the same time. I was in the car watching when it all popped off," I told her.

"What are you going to do about the police?" she asked.

"I don't know, Candy?" I said. Candy stood up and walked to the shelf and picked up a pack of cigarettes and a lighter. She lit a cigarette and tossed the pack and lighter to me.

"My name is not Candy! It's Valerie! Smooth made me say that my name was Candy," she said as she exhaled a cloud of smoke. It seemed like the more I found out about her, the less I knew. I didn't know what to say. I lit a cigarette and shook my head.

"I think I'm just going to tell them that I noticed someone following me, and slipped out of the room on the first chance I had," I told her.

"What about the diamonds?" she asked.

"I know somebody who might be able to help me move them, but I need to wait a while and let everything blow over," I said as I stubbed out my cigarette in an ashtray on the table.

For a second I wondered if she would try to set me up for the diamonds. I thought about where I should stash them, and decided that I was going to need to get a safe deposit box at the bank. I got up and went to the refrigerator to see if the beers were still there. They were, I grabbed one and walked out of the house to my car.

I was back in my neck of the woods. I wasn't in Vegas anymore and I had resources. I went to the car and grabbed my own cell phone. When I turned it on there were a lot of new messages. I didn't even bother with the voicemail messages. I went straight to the text messages.

The first message I answered was from Pretty Tony, a pimp from Detroit, who I knew had the 411 on what was going on. As soon as he answered I felt a sense of relief.

"Nephew, I see that you're among the living. Good shit my nigga! I need you to come where we usually go, so we can fix your situation my little pimp nigga!" he said to me. I knew immediately that he was telling me to come to the strip. I also knew that he was probably aware of everything the lick had consisted of. Before I hung up the phone I told him that I needed help moving some special cargo and he told me not to worry.

I hung up the phone and went back into the house. When I came back into the house the sound of SWV singing *"Weak"* made me feel even more at ease. I walked into the kitchen and stopped dead in my tracks. Valerie was standing in the doorway between the kitchen and the dining area wearing a pink see through Teddy. She had lit candles and gave me a look that told me I had no choice but to give it to her.

I walked in and sat my beer on the counter. I grabbed her and pulled her close to me as I kissed her slowly and tenderly. I pushed her against the wall and grabbed her leg to put it around my waist. I unbuckled my pants and dropped them to the floor. We made love all the way into the bedroom where I made her get on all four's and finished the job.

We lay there motionless and not saying a word. The sound of her heavy breathing told me that I had given her a run for her money. She was out for the count. I got up and walked into the bathroom. I got into the walk in shower and turned the water on as hot as I could get it. I let the heat from the water, the steam, and the sound of the music from the radio wash away all of the problems from the world. By the time I got out of the shower all I needed was a Kush blunt and a fresh beer.

I called one of my pimp buddies from the strip and asked him to drop me off the best weed he could find. A half an hour later he pulled up in front of the house and called my phone. When I saw the caller ID I jumped up and went to the front of the house to meet him.

"What's happnin nephew? Word on the streets is you been playing around with some dangerous muthafucka's!" Trife said as I got into the car. Trife was true to his name. The only thing he cared about was his reputation. His reputation was that anything was for sale for the right price.

"I need you to keep me on the cool Unc!" I told him. "I'm out here fucked up behind some shit my cousin pulled on some Russians," I said.

"You know how shit goes nephew! If you breakin bread, nobody that's eatin wit you can talk because they have full mouths. But if you're not feedin the lions you gotta know they can easily turn on you! Do you feel where I'm coming from nephew?" he said to me. I sat there for a second contemplating what I should do. After a quick thought I opened the door and told him I had something for him.

I walked to my car and popped the trunk. I opened the bag of diamonds and dumped a few in my hand. I reached into my pocket and took out the money from the heist. I peeled off a thousand dollars and put the rest back into my pocket. I walked back over and got back into the car.

When I was back in the car I handed him the diamonds. I told him they were a gift then handed him the money and told him the money was to keep me low key. He pulled out a jar that had some weed in it that was so green that it almost looked neon. He rolled a blunt and handed it to me.

"I never saw you nephew! As far as the stones go I got somebody to get rid of those for you. Smooth was my nigga! He told me that you were family and this is how families function," he said as I lit the blunt. When I tried to pass the blunt to him he pushed my hand away.

"Nephew you got too much shit goin on! Smoke that to the head and remember that family looks out for family!" he told me as he put the car into gear. "Oh yeah if you get a chance tell baby girl that all is forgiven. I couldn't stand that punk ass nigga she was wit but I got love for you nephew. I'll be in touch."

He reached into the middle console and pulled out a chrome plated 9 mm. He handed it to me and told me to watch my back. He told me that if I needed him or the homies to call but only if I had no other choice.

I walked back up the driveway wondering how much he really knew. I stopped at the car and grabbed my bag. Family or not he had seen where I was hiding my stash and I wasn't about to get caught slipping. I knew that rule number one was that nobody would set you up worse than family.

I walked back into the house and locked the door. I turned off the lights and went to the bedroom. Valerie lay there in her pink teddy sprawled out on the bed looking delicious. I got into the bed and started kissing her body until she woke up. We made love better than any of the times we ever had. When we were done we both collapse on the bed and fell asleep.

Chapter 16
Easy Like Sunday Morning

The smell of bacon frying hit my nose before I even opened my eyes. At first I thought I was back at home on a Sunday morning. I could almost feel the presence of my family in the house. I opened my eyes and my surroundings didn't look familiar.

I was in a king sized bed with flower prints all over the comforter. I looked at the dresser and saw my clothes neatly folded and waiting for me. I lifted the comforter and got out of the bed, I was naked and I couldn't remember where I was.

I put on my boxers and walked to the door way. All of a sudden I knew exactly where I was and what I had done last night. Valerie was in the kitchen cooking us breakfast. She was wearing a short silk robe. The morning sun beams lit her face as she stood by the sink looking out of the window into the back yard.

"Good morning pretty lady," I said as I walked up behind her. She turned around and hugged me. She kissed me on my cheek and turned to walk away. She was beautiful. She could definitely pass for Gabrielle Union's sister. Her high cheek bones and perky brown eyes made her smile look angelic.

"Have you ever been to Church?" she asked as she went to the stove to stir the scrambled eggs.

"Of course I have. Why do you ask?" I asked as I grabbed a piece of bacon from a plate that was sitting on the counter by the stove.

"I want you to come to church with me. After all of the bullshit I have been through lately I just want to hear a good sermon and say my prayers in person," she said.

"Okay we can do that if you can take me around afterwards to tie up some loose ends," I told her. She agreed and seemed very happy that I had decided to go to church with her. I walked up behind her and kissed her on the neck. I started to nibble on her ear and she turned around to face me.

"Don't start something that we can't finish!" she said with a smile. She put her hand on my cheek and gave me a seductive look. "Save it for later baby I don't even think I can take anymore. Get showered breakfast is almost done," she said as she gave me a shove. I walked away thinking to myself that I was going to need to be very careful with this girl. She could easily make a man want to settle down, and I wasn't ready for that.

We pulled up to a small white church with a full parking lot. The marquee in front of the church caught my eye. In big black letters the marquee read: God gives and forgives, man gets and forgets. In small red letters at the bottom of the marquee it said: FREE PRAYER HERE!

When we walked in the service had already started. The choir stood at the front of the church wearing white robes with gold trim. They had just finished singing "*God is trying to tell you something*" as we took our seat in a pew near the back of the church. A young boy moved to the front of the choir. The church band started playing a slow melody. When the boy started singing I could hardly believe his voice. He had a very powerful singing voice.

"Jesus keep me near the cross, there's a fountain; free to all a healing stream, flows from Calvary's mountain." The choir began to circle the church clapping to the beat. A girl, who couldn't have been more than 10 years old, stood next to the boy who was singing. Her voice was just as powerful as she sang.

"Near the cross I watch and wait, hoping and trusting ever; 'til I reach that golden strand, it's just beyond the river." The rest of the choir came down from the back of the church through the aisles singing and clapping to the beat.

"In the cross, in the cross be my glory ever; 'til my raptured soul shall find, one of these days I'll find rest, rest beyond the river." By the end of the song the entire congregation was on their feet singing along and clapping to the beat. The preacher walked on stage wearing a gold robe with white trim. He walked to the center of the stage as the music died down and started to speak.

"Hallelujah brothers and sisters! Can I hear the congregation say Amen?" he said. The congregation screamed out: "Amen!"

CLARK KENT

"I came here today with something on my heart today saints. You see… I met a young man this week from the streets of our neighborhood. When I pulled up to the stop light, I saw this young man robbing another young man… At first I didn't know what to do… Part of me wanted to call the police, but something in my heart told me to reach out to this young man and try to help him… I pulled my car to the curb and got out… He immediately turned the gun on me and the young man he was trying to rob took off running. The young man came closer to me still pointing his gun at me… I asked him if he believed in God and he looked at me with a curios look in his eyes… He lowered the gun and ran away… I didn't try to catch him I just watched as he ran… I wanted to tell him that he still had a chance to ask for forgiveness! I come here today to ask each one of you to turn to your neighbor and tell him or her that God forgives! Isaiah 43 verses 25 through 26 says: 'I! Even I! Am he that bloweth out thy transgressions for mine own sake, and will not remember thy sins!' Psalms 103 verse 12 says: 'As far as the east is from the west, so far hath he removed our transgressions from us…' Saints I want you to know that you have to confess your sins and be cleansed of the things that you may have done in the past. Repent ye therefore, and be converted, that your sins may be blotted out, when the times of refreshing shall come from the presence of the Lord!" he said from the pulpit. It seemed like he was talking directly to me. As he talked I could feel his message in my soul.

I looked over at Valerie and she was crying. The entire congregation seemed glued to their seats and there was no one who didn't look like they couldn't feel every word he was saying. A lady in the front row stood up and screamed hallelujah. The congregation started clapping. The preacher raised his hand and the congregation calmed down.

"Come now... And let us reason together, saith the Lord, though your sins be as scarlet, they shall be as white as snow, though they be red as crimson, they shall be as wool. If ye be willing and obedient, ye shall eat of the good of the land. Can I get a witness? Hallelujah! And now why tarriest thou? Arise and be baptized, and wash away thy sins, calling on the name of the Lord," he said. Behind him people came onto the stage wearing all white robes. The choir stated to sing again and people started lining up by the stairs to the stage. Valerie got up and stood in line as well.

I sat glued to my seat. I almost wanted to join them, but I sat and watched as people went up one at a time and got baptized. My eyes started to tear up and I began praying in my heart that God would forgive me for the drive by shootings I had done. I got up and walked out of the church.

I didn't want people seeing me so emotional. I walked to the car and sat on the hood. I put my head in my hands and wept for a short moment, then, I got myself together and went back inside.

Valerie was on the stage with a white robe on standing in a pool of water with the preacher. He put his hand on her head and said a prayer then she was pushed down backwards into the water. When she came up the congregation yelled hallelujah and she continued off of the stage.

CLARK KENT

As I sat in the back pew I thought about my cousin Smooth. I thought about how he had never known his father. How he would never have the chance to have children. I thought about how tragically Jersey had lost her life. It seemed like the people who wanted success the most and did what they had do to achieve it always died before they could ever grasp it.

I didn't know whether to feel bad that they were gone, or happy that they didn't have to deal with all this bullshit anymore. I thought about race and all of the tension that it came with; and it all seemed pointless. I asked myself what I would say if I found out that there could only be one thing that I would be remembered for. I laughed to myself at my answer. I can tell you that if I could only be remembered for one thing that it definitely wouldn't be the color of my skin.

I needed to find something that I could do with my life that I would be proud to be remembered for. I decided that I was going to go back to school and get my GED. I needed to become something. I decided that it was time to quit blaming my circumstances on racial issues, the government or anything else. It was time to grow up.

Chapter 17

Loose Ends

After church we went back to Valerie's house to change clothes. I needed to make some calls and tie up some loose ends. I needed to get in touch with a few people who owed me money. I also needed to get in touch with Pretty Tony about the diamonds.

Two hours later we left Valerie's house in her car with the top down. I was feeling pretty good. Going to church had helped to sort of clear my mind. I hadn't had a conversation with God in years. The sermon on forgiveness had taken some of the pressure off of me as well.

I pulled up to my aunt's house in Newport Beach at about four o'clock. Her house was beautiful. Her front yard had flower beds along the perimeter that lined the walkway to her front door. On the way up the walk I looked up and saw her standing on the balcony. She smiled and told us to come inside.

We walked in and took the spiral staircase to the second floor. She had it set up like a café. There were three tall black bar tables with matching bar chairs sitting on the balcony that looked out at the ocean. All around the railing to her patio she had beautiful plants. On one of the tables there were photo albums lying open. I looked at the picture on the top of the stack, it was me and Smooth standing in front of a sliding board carrying buckets and shovels. I could still remember the day the picture was taken. I picked up the picture and looked at it for a second. The day that the picture had been taken I was only five years old.

I introduced Valerie to my aunt then pulled my aunt in for a hug. She immediately broke down and started crying. We sat with my aunt for awhile looking at pictures and reminiscing. My aunt got up and told me that there was something of Smooth's that she wanted me to have.

She came back into the room carrying a cardboard box. She handed me the box and told me that what ever Smooth had in the box was very important to him. She asked that I wait until I was alone to open it.

I told my aunt that I wanted to be a pallbearer and that if there was anything she needed I wanted her to call me right away. I hugged her again and kissed her on the cheek.

"Ace, be careful out there baby. I don't want to have to bury you too!" she said as she walked us to the door.

"Auntie I think I'm about to give up this craziness out here in California," I told her. We walked to the car and I sat the box on the back seat. My aunt stood in the door and watched as we pulled off. I felt bad for her. One of her sons was doing a ten year sentence and the other was dead.

My phone rang and I looked at the caller ID. It was Pretty Tony. I turned down the music and answered the phone.

"Nephew, I got some good news for you. I'm going to be handling some business later today but if you get a chance to go where we met up last time you'll be happy to see me," he said as soon as I answered. Pretty Tony always spoke in codes. If you didn't know him you would never figure out what he was talking about. I however had gotten pretty good at figuring out what his codes meant.

He was telling me that he had a buyer for the diamonds, and that he wanted me to meet him in the parking lot of the strip club as soon as I could get there. I told Valerie that we needed to get back out to Hollywood ASAP.

When we pulled up I had Valerie park the car around the corner from the club. I found Pretty Tony sitting in a new Escalade smiling when we walked up. We got in and he pulled off. Once we were out of the strip club parking lot I showed him the bag of diamonds.

He looked at them as if he had already known what they were going to look like. He handed the bag back to me and told me we needed to speak in private. We pulled around the corner and I told Valerie to follow us in her car so we could speak in private.

Once Valerie was out of the car Pretty Tony told me that he had found out that Smooth had gotten set up by somebody on the inside. He told me to watch Candy because she might have been the one who set Smooth up.

He took the diamonds and told me that he would call me later when he was ready for me to pick up the money. He told me to make Candy think that I was still carrying around the diamonds and not let her know what was going on. He said that if she was the one who had set Smooth up that she was probably going to try to set me up too. If she did I was going to be ready.

When I got back into the car with Valerie she immediately asked if I had sold the diamonds. I told her that I showed them to him and he had said he would ask around. I was beginning to look at her in a different light. I had her take me to Englewood to pick up some money from a guy who ran a recording studio, then to Long Beach to pick up some money from some young Crips that I had fronted a few ponds of weed.

We went back to Riverside to wait for Pretty Tony to call me. When we pulled onto her street I noticed an unmarked police cruiser sitting in her driveway. I had her circle the block so I could get out in the alley behind her house then sent her to see what the police were doing at her house.

From the alley I could hear the conversation between Valerie and the detective. He was asking about Diamond. They still hadn't located a next of kin, and the detective was asking if she knew anyone who might have information about her family. She told him that they only knew each other from the strip club and that the trip to Vegas had been the first time they had ever hung out together.

Once the detective was gone I hopped the wall and went into the house through the back door. I started to wonder if she had actually set Smooth up. I thought about how she had told me that he had basically kidnapped her. That alone would be a good motive to set him up. Valerie came in through the front door carrying mail, and looking like she had something on her mind.

"I have a question. Do you think Smooth and Diamond might have gotten set up?" I asked. She looked at me with a curious look in her eyes.

"What do you mean? I mean it is definitely a possibility, but who would've been able to pull it off? Think about it if they had gotten set up by someone who wanted the diamonds wouldn't they be looking for us by now?" she replied.

Now I really suspected that she was in on it. She was right, and I was starting to believe that the reason no one was looking for us was because she already thought she had me where she wanted me. I had to come up with a way to find out. I walked to the refrigerator and grabbed a beer, then went to sit on the couch and think of a way to find out if she had been the one to set Smooth up.

I thought about how she had pulled a gun on me when she asked if I knew she had been kidnapped. I wondered if it had just been her way of tricking me into believing that she didn't set Smooth up. Once I was finished with my beer I decided it was time to leave. I went to her car and got the box that my aunt had given me and put it into the Magnum then went inside to say goodbye.

When I told her I was leaving she begged me not to go without her. I told her I needed to finish tying up some loose ends and that I would call her when I was done. She grabbed my hand and told me that she was afraid to be alone. I didn't believe her, if anything it made me even more suspicious of her. I knew that if she was responsible for the set up she wouldn't tell me no matter what I did.

I left and told her I would call her later.

Chapter 18

Take the Money and Run!

Pretty Tony called me an hour after I left Valerie's house in Riverside. He told me he had the money but we needed to meet up somewhere discreet. I decided to have him meet me at Mimi's café in Corona. When I pulled into the parking lot Pretty Tony was already there. I parked next to him and got out of the car.

"What's good pimpin?" he said as I climbed into the front seat of his truck.

"Aint nothing good but the pimpin and that ain't easy either," I told him.

"Let's get down to business nephew. Listen, because the cargo was still smoking I had to drop the price some. After my finders fee I got you $500,000. I took a quarter for movin em," he said as he handed me a small suit case. I knew I could trust him so I didn't even bother counting it. "I also checked into that situation, and found out that it's bigger than I thought. Candy is innocent but the word on the streets is that the Russians have a hit out on her. They are looking for you too nephew. You need to snatch her up and hit the road for a few tics."

"How much info do they have unc?" I asked.

"I heard that they been showin pictures. They don't know government names, but they been to the strip club twice askin bitches about y'all. I can throw some curveballs and misdirect em but they got enough power to locate you if you're not careful. My advice... Call T and B... Take a trip... Get away. Give me some time to get rid of em," he said.

I told him I was as good as gone and got out of the truck. I walked back to the Magnum and pulled off. While I was driving, I thought about what he had said. If she was innocent that changed some things.

I called Valerie and told her I wanted to take her out to dinner. I told her not to worry about what to wear because we were going shopping. I didn't tell her but my trip to Vegas had brought me a total of $700,000 and I felt like celebrating. On my way back to her house I stopped by the car lot that Jersey had taken me to where her step father had given us the Cadillac. I needed something a little classier to roll in.

When I walked into his office Jersey's step father greeted me with a smile and a hand shake. He opened his desk and pulled out a bottle of scotch and two shot glasses. We talked for awhile about missing Jersey. He told me that he had been going every Sunday to put roses on her grave. After a couple of shots he got up and looked out of the window.

"So what can I do for you?" he asked. I told him what I wanted and he fixed me up with a pretty silver Lexus. I paid him cash and told him I would be back for the Magnum. When I left the car lot I stopped at AMPM to fill up the tank, then I went to go get Valerie. I liked the new Lexus much more than the Magnum. The ride was smooth.

When I pulled up to Valerie's house I decided it would be best to park in the alley behind her house. I didn't want any of the neighbors to see the car in case the Russians came looking for us. Valerie came to the door in a towel. I could hear Luther Vandross playing on the radio inside.

As soon as I walked into the kitchen she jumped into my arms and started kissing me. I picked her up and put her on the counter as I began to take off my pants. I pulled the towel off of her and started kissing her neck and nibbling on her ear lobes. Now that I knew that she was innocent I really wanted her. We made love in almost every room in her house. When we were done I just laid there staring at her pretty face.

She was beautiful. I watched her as she slept and said a silent prayer thanking God that she hadn't been the one to set up Smooth. I was starting to like her. I mean I wasn't falling in love or anything but it was starting to look like things could get serious if I wasn't careful.

I got up and went into the bathroom for a quick shower. When I got out of the shower I looked at my phone and noticed a missed call from Pretty Tony. I called him back and found out that the Russians had found out where Valerie lived. We had to go and we had to do it in a hurry.

I woke Valerie up and told her what was going on and that we needed to leave right away. She put the Mustang in the garage and closed the garage door. As we left through the back she set the alarm so that if anybody broke in the alarm company would call the police. We had grabbed as much of what she needed as we could including the gun she had pulled on me. We wouldn't be coming back any time soon.

When we got in the car I decided it was time to call the big guns. If the Russians were looking for me I decided that I would have someone looking for them. I picked up the phone and called my crew from Watts. An hour later we met up at bar in Riverside.

"What it do big baby?" B said as he slid into the booth across from us. His brother came and sat down next to him. "I hear you need to get some hounds off yo trail in a hurry," he said with a grin. B was six foot four and about 300 pounds. His brother T was just about the same size. They were black and Philippino and they could have easily been someone's offensive ends. They were the ones who you wanted watching your back when things got rough.

I slid a yellow envelope across the table and he quickly grabbed it and put it into the pocket of his hoodie. We hadn't discussed a price but I knew from past experiences about how much they'd want.

"Pretty Tony has more info than I do about the hounds. From what I hear they been askin' around on the track and supposedly they found out where baby girl lives," I told him as I sipped my drink.

"Give us the keys to the house and lay low until you hear me. I got this fam!" B said as the waitress walked up to take our order. I bought a round of drinks for us but told the waitress we didn't want to order food. Valerie and I were about to have a good night on the town. Once the waitress was gone Valerie gave him her keys and the code for the alarm. We said "cheers" and downed the shots. They got up and I stood up to shake hands with them as they left. I knew that I didn't have anything else to worry about. I had just paid them $100,000 to get rid of the Russians and I knew that it was guaranteed.

T and B were known for their ability to solve problems for people. Their real names were Terry and Barry but no one knew them by anything but T and B. They were ready for their mission. The first thing they were going to do was go back to the house they had been given keys to and wait to see if the so called Russian crew would actually show up.

They didn't plan to hide out at all. In fact they were going to have the lights on and make it look like the people who lived there were home. They had enough fire power to take out a police station and they would be ready at a seconds notice. While B was setting up the motion activated cameras T was ordering pizza and unloading the guns from their SUV.

They were armed with two pistol grip door breacher twelve gage shotguns, two tech nine semi automatics and two nine millimeter handguns. They decided to turn off the lights downstairs after the pizza had been delivered and wait in the dark. The only lights on in the house were the bedroom lights.

"Ok we're good bro," Barry said once everything was set up.

"Stay away from the fucking windows bro. And make sure you got the cameras on," Terry said as he moved the couch to give him a better view of the front of the house.

"Trust me Bro if anything out there moves we'll know before they do," Terry said as he opened the laptop and sat it on the floor in front of the window. They were ready. If anybody came to this house they were guaranteed to die.

"Hey Bro you watch the front of the house and I'll set up in the kitchen watching the back," Barry said.

"I got cameras set up all around we'll know if somebody comes bro," Terry told him as he turned the laptop around for his brother to see. "This fucking pizza is bomb tho bro."

"I'm taking one of those pizzas and watching the back. You just make sure you're watching that stupid fucking screen bro," Terry said as he grabbed one of the pizza boxes from the table. At first there wasn't really any activity at all but by 10:30 the first signs of someone scoping out the house were became noticeable.

A black Lincoln pulled up and parked across the street from the house. Another black car drove past and stopped at the end of the street. T and B saw the set up and were ready for action. The door to the Lincoln opened and a big Russian climbed out. T had positioned himself at the front window and B was near the front door. The first floor of the house was dark and they sat in the shadows waiting.

The Russian walked onto the porch and knocked on the door. The second time that he knocked T answered with a blast from the pistol grip. The force from the blast left a hole the size of a basketball in the door and sent the Russian flying off of the porch. The doors of the Lincoln opened and three more Russians ran towards the house with guns drawn.

Barry stood up from his position in front of the window started shooting. The windows crashed and the bullets bounced off of the Lincoln. One of the Russians fired back as they continued to move on the house. The black car that had been parked at the end of the street peeled rubber and sped up beside the Lincoln and three more Russians got out using the car for cover.

Gunshots blasted from inside the house as the first three Russians came towards the house. The front door flew open and T lit up the porch with the pistol grip. All three of the Russians went down. Barry opened fire on the car that had pulled up beside the Lincoln shooting out windows on both cars.

One of the Russians ran from the cover of the car and sprayed the front of the house with an Uzi. He ducked behind a tree and let off three more short bursts from the Uzi towards the front door. Barry let off five shots from the 9 mm and dropped the Russian on the front lawn. The gunfire stopped and the remaining two Russians got back into the black car and sped off. T and B grabbed their guns and fled out of the back door towards the SUV. Once they were sure they had everything they pulled off down the alley. They knew it would only be a matter of time before the area was crawling with police. Their job was done for the night.

Chapter 19

The Wash

We left the bar in Riverside and I decided to go against my better judgment and take Veronica to my spot in Redondo Beach. My general rule was that I never brought anybody back to my place. It was the one place where I knew no one could find me. The only person who even knew me in the area was the owner of the house. I was renting the attic apartment and the only way in was through his house.

I pulled into the parking lot by the beach and parked the car. We got out and took a walk along the beach. While we were walking I decided it was time to get to know Valerie a little better. The first thing I wanted to know was if it was true that she used to be Pimpin Ken's bottom bitch.

I couldn't think of any other way than to just outright ask her. "So is it true?" I asked.

"Is what true?" she replied looking kind of quizzical.

"That you used to be Pimpin Ken's bottom bitch?" I asked. She let go of my hand and sat down in the sand looking at the water.

"Yeah... I was with Kenny before I met Derek," she said as I sat down beside her. I could tell I had struck a nerve. Her eyes had a far away look in them as if she was envisioning another place in time. "I guess you could say I was his bottom bitch. Only he was the only one who couldn't see it. I was the one who kept his bitches in line. They didn't respect him. He had no idea what he had. All he cared about was his reputation.

He left me for dead for another bitch. That's how I met Derek. All he wanted was for me to stay out of the life and take care of him. They killed him for nothing! They took my life away from me. So yeah, it's true!" she had tears in her eyes.

I didn't speak again for awhile as I sat watching the moonlight reflect off of the waves. I had heard stories about how loyal she was to Ken. She was a down ass girl. She knew how to treat a man. I stood up and held out my hand to help her up. We walked back towards the street to find a bar or a restaurant to hang out. We found a pizza place that also served drinks and decided to go inside.

We sat in a booth and ordered a pizza and some Merlot. I told a couple of jokes to make her smile and take her mind off of her past. After we kicked it for a while we went back to the car and I took her to my place. I parked the car on the street in front of a four story beach house. The lights on the lower floors were on and I knew that Uncle Jimmy was home.

We walked up the walkway towards the door, the sound of Jazz being played in the house let me know that he was probably entertaining company. The door opened and Uncle Jimmy came out carrying a bottle of wine and a wine glass. He was drunk! I introduced Valerie to him and he motioned for us to go inside.

Uncle Jimmy owned a limousine company. Big time pimps used his limos to move dates around. If a client was coming into town for a business meeting, Jimmy's limos would be at the airport to pick them up and provide safe transportation for them. He was a cool old dude.

Once we were inside he poured us glasses of wine and came into the living room. In addition to having a limo service he was also the man who knew everything that was happening in the city.

"I figured you would be here tonight. I heard the whole story boy. You came to the right place though," he said as he sat down on one of the couches across from us. Right away I could tell that he already knew Valerie. She seemed more relaxed now that we were with him.

"Unc I need to wash some money," I said as I sipped my wine.

"I know nephew. That's already in the works. Shit I knew before you did. Who do you think set the whole ball in motion? I also know who set my boy up! I'm just glad you didn't get killed up there too."

"Shit you and me both, I wasn't even up there for that. I didn't find out till he got there," I told him.

"You can't run with the money Ace. I'm just glad you gave the diamonds to the right person. Smooth was supposed to bring the diamonds to Pretty Tony anyway. The money is to be split three ways. Originally it was me, Smooth, and Tony. Tony took his cut and the rest is a two way split between us," he said with a smile. I knew he was going to tax me for washing the money but I had no idea he was going to want half.

"Candy, thank you my dear you were very helpful as well," he said as he stood up to leave the room. I was pissed. She had been playing me all along. I wasn't going to let myself get upset or show any emotion on the subject. I got up and led Candy upstairs to my apartment. I opened the door and walked straight to the kitchen to get a beer. Candy came inside and closed the door. I walked to the patio and slid open the glass door. The smell of the ocean and the sound of the waves splashing always helped to calm me. I sat down in one of the chairs on the porch and sipped my beer.

Everything I had just learned had blown my mind. In a sense it was funny that without even knowing I had gotten the diamonds back to where they were originally supposed to go. Then my mind shifted to thoughts of Smooth. He had died before he ever got out of Vegas. I thought about the fact that Uncle Jimmy had set the heist up and wondered how much of a coincidence it really was that Candy had stuck by my side.

All of this had happened just from me wanting to go to Vegas to remember Jersey. I laughed to myself thinking about how much Jersey would've loved every minute of this Vegas trip. She would've been by my side every step of the way. Then I thought about Candy who had actually been there in place of Jersey.

I thought about all of the times we had made love during the journey. She walked to the door and stuck her head out.

"Mind if I join you?" she asked.

"Make yourself at home. Don't mind me I just have a lot on my mind right now," I said as I motioned for her to sit. She sat on my lap and turned my face to look at her.

"I feel safe when I'm with you Ace. I wasn't playing you or trying to lead you in any direction. You are the only reason I made it out of Vegas. Nobody played you. Ace, you saw the situation fall apart and made sure that it went down like it was supposed to. You made the right decisions and called all of the right people because you knew how Smooth operated. If it wasn't for you, Smooth and Diamond would have died for nothing," she said with tears in her eyes. She kissed my lips then got up and stood by the railing.

Damn she was fine. Looking at her it was hard to imagine a man being able to share her with anybody let alone everybody. As much as I wanted to deny it, I was starting to like her. I stood up and grabbed her from behind. I kissed her neck and nibbled on her ear.

"I'm going to freshen up a bit and slip into something more comfortable. Would you mind bringing my bag from the car?" She asked as she wiggled out of my arms. I needed to get my own bags from the car as well. I needed to break bread with Uncle Jimmy and see just how much it had cost me to come here.

When I got the bags inside I sat all of them but one by the door. The bag I needed was the Louis Vitton suit case that contained the money. I put the bag on the bed and unzipped it.

It was full of money. A yellow envelope that contained the original $200,000 sat on top of the stacks of bills. I zipped the bag and took it down stairs.

"I had to pay T and B but other than that this is what we have," I said as I sat the bag on the couch.

"I already have your share clean and in an account for you. I wouldn't have let Smooth do it if I thought he wasn't going to be able to get the job done. He was supposed to be in and out, he had no business even being in a God damned hotel!" he said as he slammed his hand on the counter. Smooth was like his son. He had been the one looking out for Smooth. He was also the one who taught Smooth how to hustle.

"Ace, I really appreciate what you did. I don't know how in the hell you did it; not even knowing the game plan, but you scored a touch down nephew. I owe you one boy," he said as he shook my hand. I had finished the job. I felt like gong on a cruise.

About the Author

Clark Kent was born and raised in Cleveland, Ohio. His inspirations for writing include authors like Donald Goins and Ice Berg Slim. His stories are partially fictionalized, yet reflect everyday life from a different point of view.

Run!

Las Vegas

CLARK KENT

↑UPTOWN
MEDIA - JOINT VENTURES